CAMPAIGN 419

MANILA BAY 1898

Dawn of an American Empire

BRIAN LANE HERDER ILLUSTRATED BY EDOUARD A. GROULT

OSPREY PUBLISHING
Bloomsbury Publishing Plc
Kemp House, Chawley Park, Cumnor Hill, Oxford OX2 9PH, UK
Bloomsbury Publishing Ireland Limited,
29 Earlsfort Terrace, Dublin 2, D02 AY28, Ireland
1385 Broadway, 5th Floor, New York, NY 10018, USA
E-mail: info@ospreypublishing.com
www.ospreypublishing.com

OSPREY is a trademark of Osprey Publishing Ltd

First published in Great Britain in 2025

© Osprey Publishing Ltd, 2025

All rights reserved. No part of this publication may be: i) reproduced or transmitted in any form, electronic or mechanical, including photocopying, recording or by means of any information storage or retrieval system without prior permission in writing from the publishers; or ii) used or reproduced in any way for the training, development or operation of artificial intelligence (AI) technologies, including generative AI technologies. The rights holders expressly reserve this publication from the text and data mining exception as per Article 4(3) of the Digital Single Market Directive (EU) 2019/790

A catalog record for this book is available from the British Library.

ISBN: PB 9781472865427; eBook 9781472865434; ePDF 9781472865441; XML 9781472865458

25 26 27 28 29   10 9 8 7 6 5 4 3 2 1

Maps by Bounford.com
3D BEVs by Paul Kime
Index by Alison Worthington
Typeset by PDQ Digital Media Solutions, Bungay, UK
Printed by Repro India Ltd

Osprey Publishing supports the Woodland Trust, the UK's leading woodland conservation charity.

To find out more about our authors and books visit www.ospreypublishing.com. Here you will find extracts, author interviews, details of forthcoming events and the option to sign up for our newsletter.

For product safety related questions contact productsafety@bloomsbury.com

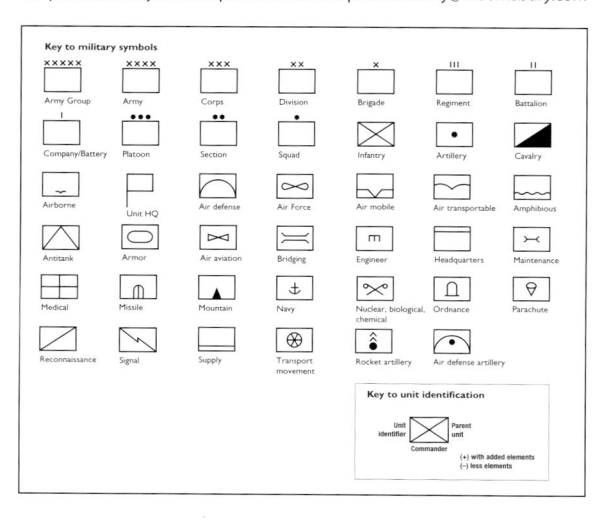

Front cover main illustration: USS *Olympia* leads the Asiatic Squadron into battle, May 1, 1898. (Edouard A. Groult)
Title page image: Painting of the May 1, 1898 battle of Manila Bay. (Muller, Luchsinger & Co., Library of Congress)

CONTENTS

ORIGINS OF THE CAMPAIGN 5
Introduction . The Kingdom of Spain: An empire in decline . The United States: A power on the rise
American influence in the Pacific, 1848–98 . The Filipino revolution, 1896–97 . The Cuban crisis, 1898

CHRONOLOGY 15

OPPOSING COMMANDERS 17
Spanish . American . Filipino

OPPOSING FORCES 22
Spanish . American . Filipino . Orders of battle

OPPOSING PLANS 32
Spanish . American . Filipino

THE CAMPAIGN 37
Prelude . The battle of Manila Bay, May 1 . The Republic of Hawai'i, March–May
Tension in Manila Bay, May–July . The US Army's Philippine Expedition is dispatched to Manila
Capture of Guam, June 20–21 . Contraalmirante Cámara's Segundo Escuadrón, May–July
War annexation of Hawai'i, July–August . Land campaign outside Manila, July–August
The battle of Manila, August 13

AFTERMATH 90
Spain . The United States . The Philippines

THE BATTLEFIELD TODAY 93

SELECT BIBLIOGRAPHY 94

INDEX 95

World map, 1898

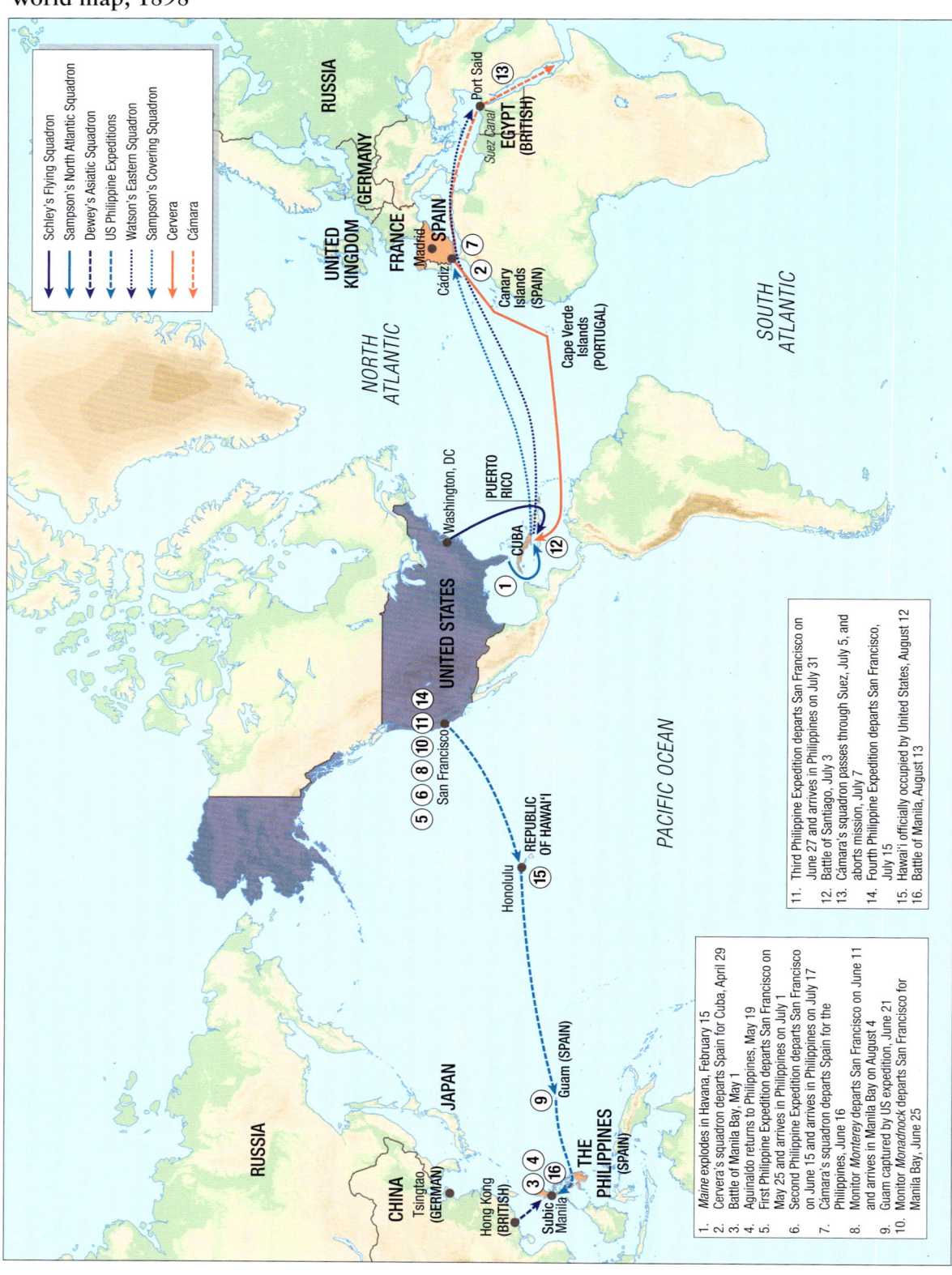

Legend:
- Schley's Flying Squadron
- Sampson's North Atlantic Squadron
- Dewey's Asiatic Squadron
- US Philippine Expeditions
- Watson's Eastern Squadron
- Sampson's Covering Squadron
- Cervera
- Cámara

1. *Maine* explodes in Havana, February 15
2. Cervera's squadron departs Spain for Cuba, April 29
3. Battle of Manila Bay, May 1
4. Aguinaldo returns to Philippines, May 19
5. First Philippine Expedition departs San Francisco on May 25 and arrives in Philippines on July 1
6. Second Philippine Expedition departs San Francisco on June 15 and arrives in Philippines on July 17
7. Cámara's squadron departs Spain for the Philippines, June 16
8. Monitor *Monterey* departs San Francisco on June 11 and arrives in Manila Bay on August 4
9. Guam captured by US expedition, June 21
10. Monitor *Monadnock* departs San Francisco for Manila Bay, June 25
11. Third Philippine Expedition departs San Francisco on June 27 and arrives in Philippines on July 31
12. Battle of Santiago, July 3
13. Cámara's squadron passes through Suez, July 5, and aborts mission, July 7
14. Fourth Philippine Expedition departs San Francisco, July 15
15. Hawai'i officially occupied by United States, August 12
16. Battle of Manila, August 13

ORIGINS OF THE CAMPAIGN

INTRODUCTION

The May 1, 1898 battle of Manila Bay is usually remembered as a single, spectacularly decisive American naval victory that extinguished a 400-year-old global empire while giving birth to the current age's global superpower – all in one day, before the sun went down, and all concentrated in just a few square miles of a single shallow tropical harbor.

In fact, the May 1, 1898 naval battle was just one part of a grand, sweeping theater of war that geographically stretched from the US West Coast all the way to Hong Kong, encompassing the full breadth of the planet's largest single surface feature, and even involved dueling (albeit aborted) naval offensives across the Atlantic and through the Suez Canal to effect a final resolution to the Manila Bay problem. Multiple islands and landmasses saw the organized ground forces of at least three different nations engaged to secure a lush smattering of dry land lapped by Asiatic seas.

The entire campaign is struck through by a vibrant streak of the surreal. The decisive land battle of Manila, the war's climax, was actually a mutually

The May 1, 1898 battle of Manila Bay was one of the most decisive actions in history. Although it did not bring about the downfall of the Spanish Empire by itself, it put into motion events that essentially doomed the Kingdom of Spain's ability to retain its last major overseas holdings. (Muller, Luchsinger & Co., Library of Congress, hereafter LOC)

choreographed sham battle between two armies that inadvertently became an unpredictable real battle between three armies. Indeed, the US Army's August 13, 1898 attack on Intramuros, Manila's walled old city, was likely the last time a war between two modern Western nations was decided by an assault on a stone fortification.

Moreover, in temporal terms, the severe political and cultural causes and consequences of the Manila naval battle stretch many decades both forwards and backwards from May 1, 1898. Literally all the landmasses the belligerents contested in 1898 would again be fought over, viciously, between 1941 and 1945. In short, the battle of Manila Bay was not merely the isolated naval battle it has so often been made out to be – it ushered in the very first Pacific War and set the stage for an ominous sequel to culminate near the end of the first half of the 20th century.

THE KINGDOM OF SPAIN: AN EMPIRE IN DECLINE

The Spanish Empire had begun in 1492, when Christopher Columbus's first expedition landed in the New World. Over the next three centuries, this initial Spanish foothold would expand to dominate most of the Caribbean and Central America, half of South America, and much of North America.

By the mid-1500s, Spanish power had begun pushing into the Pacific. In 1565, a Spanish expedition led by Miguel López de Legazpi officially claimed the island of Guam for Spain, and began colonizing the Philippine archipelago, naming the latter after Spain's ruling King Philip II. On May 19, 1571, Legazpi's Spaniards and allies permanently conquered the Philippines' largest city, Manila, ultimately ensuring Manila's prestige as capital of the Spanish East Indies and of the Philippines itself.

However, between 1808 and 1814, the Kingdom of Spain was occupied and ravaged during the Napoleonic Wars, which greatly weakened Spanish prestige. Most of Spain's American colonies would win independence by 1824. Afterwards, only Cuba, Puerto Rico, the Philippines, and the Caroline, Mariana, and Marshall islands remained Spanish possessions.

THE UNITED STATES: A POWER ON THE RISE

The United States' 1898 population was about 75 million – four times Spain's 18 million. Although predominantly Protestant, the United States was a secular democracy where both freedom of religion and the separation of church and government were enshrined into its constitution. Despite its significant Catholic minority, American society largely viewed Spain as being especially backward and papist – the worst of Old World values.

By 1898, the United States' Gross National Product (GNP) was about $22 billion, compared to $1.8 billion for Spain, a calculated 12:1 advantage for the United States, while the average American was three times more productive than the average Spaniard.

However, by the 1890s, the young, vibrant, and economically powerful United States was suffering a sudden identity crisis. In 1890, the US government declared the 400-year conquest of the American frontier complete. That same year, the United States overtook Great Britain as the world's largest economy. However, with the internal empire-building of a continent suddenly fulfilled, no virgin markets remained to populate or exploit, which 19th-century economic theory believed crucial to sustaining a dynamic economy. Almost imperceptibly, US intellectual and business elites began looking outwards to continue the so-called Manifest Destiny of American economic and cultural expansion.

AMERICAN INFLUENCE IN THE PACIFIC, 1848–98

The United States had first established sovereignty on the Pacific Ocean in 1848, having purchased California from Mexico as spoils of the recent Mexican War. Then in 1856, the Guano Islands Act began the concept of American "Insular Areas" – outlying islands claimed by the United States but not part of it. So long as an island was unoccupied and under no other national jurisdiction, it could be legally claimed for the United States. In the Pacific, Baker Island and Howland Island were occupied in 1857 under the Guano Islands Act, followed by Johnston Atoll and Jarvis Island in 1858. Kingman Reef was occupied the subsequent year, followed by Midway Atoll, which was formally occupied in 1867. All were seen as stepping stones to China, a seemingly bottomless market ripe for economic exploitation.

The Kingdom of Hawai'i, 1795–1893

On January 18, 1778, members of a Royal Navy expedition under Captain James Cook had become the first Europeans to discover the Hawai'ian islands, a major but isolated volcanic archipelago strategically located deep in the central Pacific. Beginning in 1795, an indigenous warrior

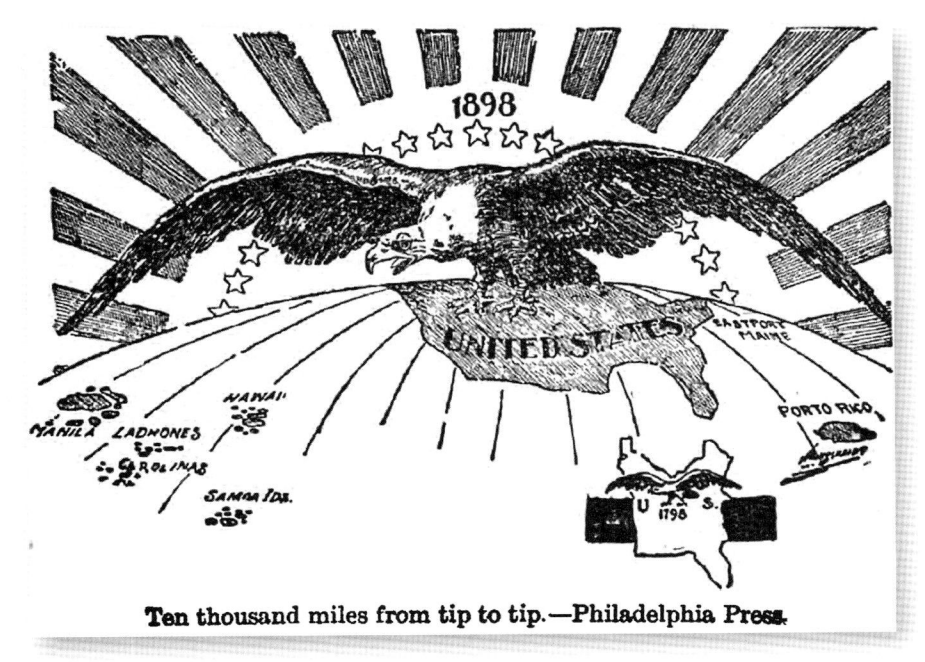

An 1899 political cartoon portrays the American eagle projecting its wings over the sudden new American empire, claiming "Ten thousand miles from tip to tip." The stark change from a built-in continental nation to European-style overseas possessions was a controversial new issue to deal with. (Attributed to "Philadelphia Press," public domain, via Wikimedia Commons)

chief, Kamehameha I, waged a 15-year campaign that unified the islands of Hawaiʻi, Oʻahu, Maui, Molokaʻi, Lanaʻi, and Kauaʻi into the Kingdom of Hawaiʻi (Aupuni Moʻi o Hawaiʻi). King Kamehameha had been greatly assisted by Western weapons and advisors, and now established Hawaiʻi's government as a constitutional monarchy in the style of a modern liberal European state.

Britain and France formally recognized Hawaiʻi in November 1843, making Hawaiʻi the first non-European indigenous state recognized by any great power. Hawaiʻi's capital and main port was Honolulu, on the island of Oʻahu. Six miles west of Honolulu was Wai Momi, a large, silted-in estuary whose name translated into English as Pearl Harbor. However, the as-yet undredged Pearl Harbor was no deeper than 15ft at high tide and not yet conducive to deep-water shipping.

Ever since European contact, indigenous Hawaiʻians had found themselves increasingly decimated by smallpox, bubonic plague, mumps, measles, cholera, influenza, and venereal diseases. Between 1778 and 1823, the archipelago's indigenous population had fallen from 300,000 to 134,750, and continued to decline. Hawaiʻian political, military, and economic power collapsed accordingly.

Americans had established the first sugar plantation on Kauaʻi in 1835, and in 1849, the United States and the Kingdom of Hawaiʻi signed a treaty establishing bilateral relations. However, industrial sugar production's grueling, unskilled physical labor was an alien concept to the indigenous Polynesians. Hawaiʻi's lush, fertile islands and mild, pleasant climate had provided easy sustenance for centuries, meaning few Hawaiʻians were interested in menial work. Additionally, by 1850, the Kingdom's indigenous Hawaiʻian population had fallen to 82,035 and was still dwindling. Therefore, in 1850, the sugar plantations began importing the necessary cheap labor, largely from China and Japan.

In early 1874, anti-American riots inspired USS *Tuscarora* and USS *Portsmouth* to land naval infantry. To better entrench relations, the 1875 Reciprocity Treaty was established, allowing Hawaiʻi tariff-free sugar imports to the United States and granting Pearl Harbor to the US Navy (USN) as a concession port.

By 1887, Hawaiʻi's King David Kalākaua had become increasingly unpopular and the new so-called "Bayonet Constitution" virtually stripped Kalākaua of power while also enfranchising the vote to non-indigenous Hawaiʻians. King Kalākaua died in January 1891 and was succeeded by his daughter, Queen Liliʻuokalani.

The Republic of Hawaiʻi, 1893–98

Hawaiʻi's international trade was now overwhelmingly dependent on the United States, and had been for decades. By 1892, the last full year of the Kingdom of Hawaiʻi, 93.1 percent of Hawaiʻi's total international trade was with the United States, encompassing 81.9 percent of Hawaiʻi's imports and 99.6 percent of its exports. Led by Sanford B. Dole, the American sugar and fruit tycoons in control of Hawaiʻi's economy increasingly sought its formal annexation to the United States.

On January 17, 1893, the so-called Committee of Safety, composed of American and European businessmen, staged a coup d'état against the Hawaiʻian Kingdom. They were assisted by the Honolulu-based cruiser

USS *Boston*, which landed troops to successfully secure the Kingdom's overthrow. The new pro-American oligarchy established a Provisional Government of Hawai'i. The pro-annexation US Minister to Hawai'i, John Stevens, unilaterally proclaimed Hawai'i a US protectorate.

However, by March 1893, the US government was controlled by the anti-annexationist Democratic Party. Months of in-person lobbying by the deposed Queen Lili'uokalani ensured that US efforts to annex Hawai'i failed. Therefore, on July 4, 1894, Hawai'i's provisional government proclaimed itself the Republic of Hawai'i and officially announced the Republic's desire to be annexed by the United States. The US government formally recognized the independent Republic of Hawai'i in August 1894.

The new Republic of Hawai'i's total population was 115,000. Half spoke English and half were Christian, including many indigenous Hawai'ians. About 30,000 lived in Hawai'i's capital, Honolulu. However, only 35,000 Hawai'ians (about one-third) were indigenous Polynesians; the remaining 80,000 were non-indigenous residents. Some 50,000 were East Asian, including 25,000 Japanese and 23,000 Chinese. Another 16,000 were Portuguese. Finally, 5,000 Hawai'ians were *haole* (Northern European whites). About 2,000 *haole* were American. The remaining 3,000 *haole* were mostly Britons or Germans who increasingly identified themselves as American.

In January 1895, Republic of Hawai'i forces crushed the three-day, pro-royalist "Wilcox Rebellion," after which Queen Lili'uokalani and several ringleaders were briefly imprisoned by the Republic government.

By November 1896, pro-annexation Republicans had regained control of the US government. On June 16, 1897, the new US president, William McKinley, co-signed a tentative treaty of annexation with the Republic of Hawai'i. After months of strong royalist Hawai'ian lobbying, the February 27, 1898 vote in the US Senate fell short of the required two-thirds supermajority needed for ratification.

The crown princess and future queen of Hawai'i, Lili'uokalani, seen in London at Queen Victoria's 1887 Jubilee. Hawai'i was an entirely sovereign and internationally recognized nation for over half a century before falling under the control of the United States. (Walery [Stanislaw Julian Ostrorog (1830–90)], public domain, via Wikimedia Commons)

THE FILIPINO REVOLUTION, 1896–97

Lying in the southwestern Pacific, the Philippine archipelago comprises 7,641 islands, whose combined land area is just smaller than the state of Montana. The Philippines have traditionally been divided into three regions: the largest and northernmost island, Luzon; a central group of smaller islands, called the Visayas; and finally, the southernmost and second-largest island, Mindanao.

During this period, the Philippines was ruled by the Capitania General de Filipinas (Captaincy-General of the Philippines), which until 1821 answered to the Viceroyalty of New Spain (Mexico). After 1821, the Captaincy-General answered directly to Madrid.

The imperial powers in Southeast Asia, May 1, 1898

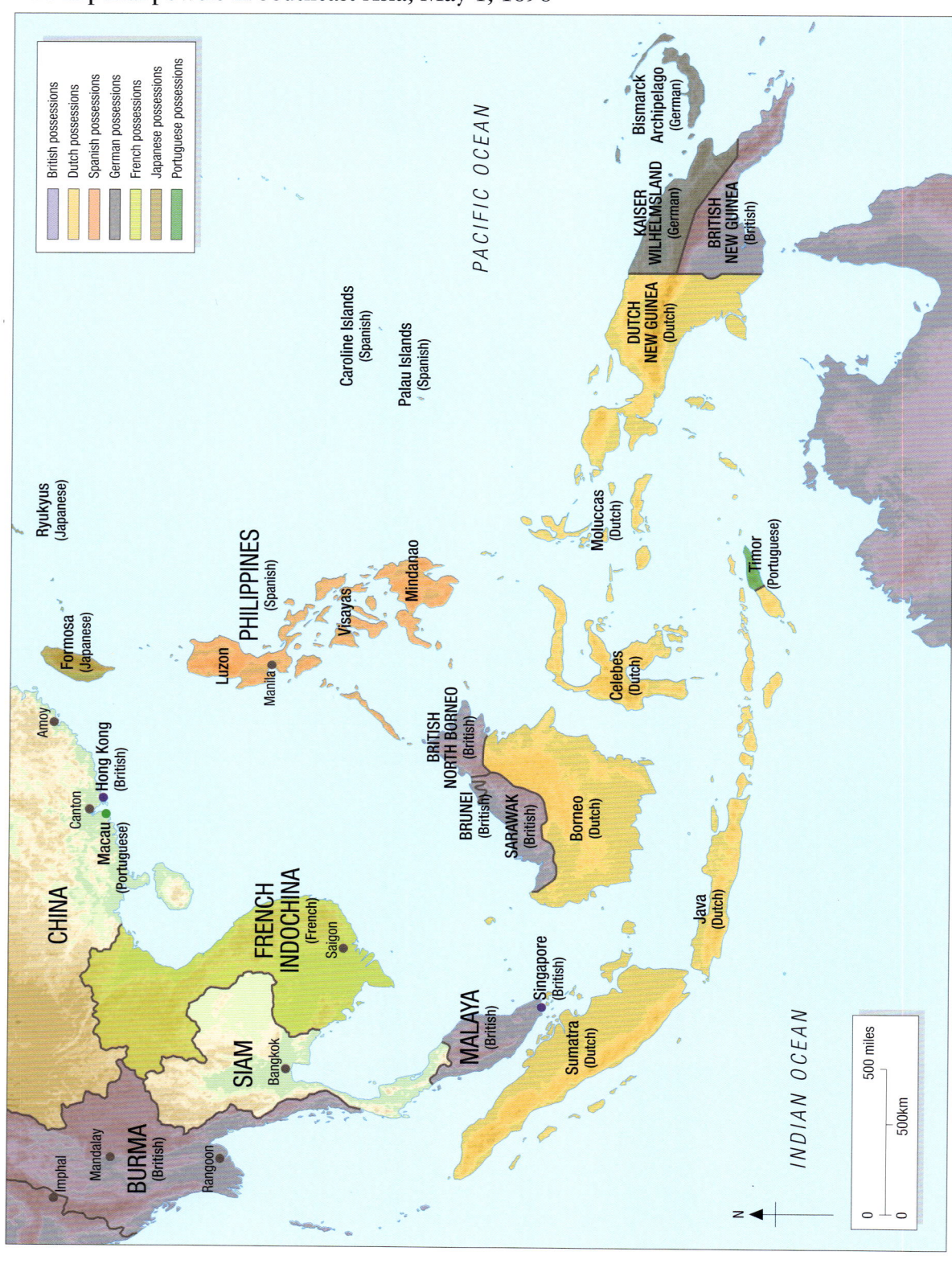

By 1898, the Philippines had a population of 7.8 million. Manila's population was about 400,000, of which 68 percent were full Filipino, 29 percent were full or mixed Chinese, and most of the remaining 3 percent were full or mixed Spanish. The *lingua franca* was Tagalog, the primary language of the Manila capital region. The ruling Spanish government in the Philippines comprised about 30,000 officials.

Except for Muslims in the south and the most remote tribes, the Filipino population had been devotedly Catholic for over 200 years. The local parish priests were well-respected, but the monastic orders of friars, who answered directly to the Pope, were greatly despised for their corruption and high-handedness. "Unlike the good men in [America]," contemporary historian Karl Irving Faust claimed, these friars "to a very great extent… were ignorant, brutish, licentious, and rapacious…" With their frequent employment in the Filipino education and civil administration systems, the friars "could and did practice all forms of petty extortion, while leading… in many cases… wholly immoral lives."

In the 1880s, a small group of progressive, European-educated, Spanish-speaking Filipino intellectuals called the Ilustrados began gaining influence in the Philippines. The Ilustrados did not seek national independence, but instead full assimilation into an idealized Spanish society that rewarded merit and disregarded ethnic background. Of these, the most prominent was José Rizal, a writer and ophthalmologist who founded the peaceful La Liga Filipina, a group that supported full Filipino representation in the Spanish Cortes (parliament) in Madrid.

However, in 1892, Filipino Andrés Bonifacio y de Castro secretly established the militant Katipunan in response to Rizal's more moderate La Liga Filipina. Unlike Rizal's group, the Katipunan's objective was complete Filipino independence through armed revolt.

In 1896, some 5,000 Filipinos signed a petition requesting that Japan annex the Philippines. The Japanese government turned this evidence over to the Spaniards. The Spanish were temporarily forced to be lenient, as they then had only 1,500 Spanish troops and 6,000 indigenous auxiliaries to garrison the whole country. Shortly afterwards, the wife of a Katipunan official confessed to a priest that the Katipunan was conspiring to slaughter all Spaniards and foreigners in the Philippines on August 20, 1896. The Spanish promptly imprisoned 300 suspects.

On August 26, 1896, the Katipunan pre-emptively declared war on Spain with the *Sigaw ng Pugad Lawin* (Cry of Pugad Lawin). Filipino insurgents raided Caloocan, killing and capturing some Chinese, before escaping ahead of Spanish cavalry. Four days later, on August 30, the insurgents attacked San Juan del Monte, just outside Manila. Eighty insurgents were killed to just one Spaniard. On September 4, 1896, the Spanish began executing insurgents captured at San Juan. The rebellion now spread like wildfire across the country, where it was universally popular with the indigenous population. Nevertheless, the revolt's many small skirmishes continued to favor the Spaniards.

However, in the province of Cavite, an eloquent, self-confident 28-year-old school teacher named Emilio Aguinaldo issued a proclamation to the Filipinos urging general resistance. Aguinaldo immediately organized the revolutionary movement in Cavite and then marched on Cavite's Imus, which he took and fortified, along with Paranaque and Las Piñas south of the Cavite fort. Aguinaldo's heavily entrenched men then repulsed a major

Ilustrado writer José Rizal, Filipino nationalist and founder of the peaceful La Liga Filipina. Rizal had volunteered his services as a doctor during the Cuban revolt but was arrested on his way home in October 1896 and executed on December 30. Rizal is now remembered as arguably the Philippines' greatest national hero. (Public domain, via Wikimedia Commons)

General Emilio Aguinaldo, circa 1898. Unlike Rizal, who was martyred by the Spanish in 1896, Aguinaldo had the misfortune to live through the extremely complex and difficult events of 1898–1901 in which a clear path to outright Filipino victory was virtually impossible. (Public domain, via Wikimedia Commons)

Spanish attack that destroyed nearly half a regiment of auxiliaries and killed an additional 50 Spanish regulars. The Spanish withdrew into their own trenches, and in Manila executed another 13 Filipino provocateurs.

The rebels by now largely besieged Manila, but despite victories at Carmona, Silan, Imus, and Binacayan, were unable to break into the city. Additionally, in the provinces of Bulacan and Pampanga north of Manila was a force of 3,000 insurgents, countered ineffectually by 500 Spanish cavalry.

Fueled by mutual racial hatred, the war so far had largely been barbarous and atrocity-ridden on both sides. Although La Liga Filipina's José Rizal was a liberal moderate completely innocent of the armed revolt, he had long been the most visible Filipino nationalist. After a sham trial, Rizal was executed by Spanish authorities on December 30, 1896.

At this point, there were 10,000 Spanish regulars in the Philippines facing 35,000 Filipino insurgents. There were now three major centers of insurrection: Bulacan under General Mariano Llanera; Morong under General Andrés Bonifacio; and in Cavite under Aguinaldo were 7,000 insurgents armed with Mauser rifles. By now, Aguinaldo controlled all of Cavite except the Cavite fort itself.

In December 1896, Philippines Governor-General Ramón Blanco was recalled to Madrid and replaced by General Camilo de Polavieja. Steadily reinforced with a combined force of 28,000 regulars and auxiliaries, Polavieja went on the offensive in Cavite, the revolutionary hotbed. On February 17, 1897, Aguinaldo's force of 10,000 insurgents ambushed Polavieja's advancing Spanish column of 16,000 troops at Zapote Bridge, Cavite, and routed them. Two days later, Polavieja renewed his offensive with 23,000 troops and began recapturing most of Cavite province.

By April 1897, Aguinaldo had united his forces with those of Llanera, and together they overran several northern provinces, including Tarlac. The Spanish retaliated, but by now the Filipino auxiliaries and priests, motivated by Spanish atrocities, were almost entirely defecting to the insurgents. The conflict had devolved into a widespread guerilla war of raids and skirmishes

The February 17, 1897 battle of Zapote Bridge, as depicted by Vicente Dizon in 1926. Led by Aguinaldo, some 10,000 insurgents, armed mostly with melee weapons, ambushed and repulsed an army of 16,000 Spanish troops. (Vicente Dizon, public domain, via Wikimedia Commons)

rather than Aguinaldo's carefully planned pitched battles.

An inevitable power struggle ensued between the overall leader, Bonifacio, and those backing the young upstart Aguinaldo. In the Katipunan's subsequent 1897 elections, Aguinaldo was elected president *in absentia*. A political crisis erupted where both sides ultimately claimed the other's political gains were illegitimate. In April 1897, Aguinaldo's backers arrested Bonifacio, found him guilty of treason, and sentenced him to death. After initially commuting Bonifacio's sentence to banishment, a reluctant Aguinaldo was ultimately persuaded to execute Bonifacio in May 1897.

By now, the current Spanish governor-general of the Philippines, Camilo de Polavieja, had found himself tiring of the constant fighting and asked to be relieved. Polavieja departed for Spain on April 15, 1897 and was replaced by Fernando Primo de Rivera. By late April, Rivera had taken military control of Spanish forces from Cavite but was dismayed at how – contrary to expectations – the Filipino insurgents were united against the Spanish. Rivera immediately decreed that any Filipino who disarmed and surrendered to Spanish authority by May 17, 1897, would be granted a full pardon. Few Filipinos responded. Rivera responded by launching an aggressive campaign against the Filipino rebels, forcing Aguinaldo and his men to withdraw to Batangas. Aguinaldo's headquarters was soon surrounded by Spanish troops, but he and 500 picked men slipped the siege and withdrew deep into the rugged Luzon heartland, setting up a new headquarters at Biak-na-Bato.

On August 6, 1897, Governor-General Rivera commissioned a Filipino official, Pedro A. Paterno, to negotiate a truce between the Spanish government and Aguinaldo's army. Aguinaldo's revolutionary demands were stated as follows:

1. The expulsion of the friars and the return to the Filipinos of the lands which they had appropriated for themselves.
2. Representation in the Spanish Cortes.
3. Freedom of the press and tolerance of all religious sects.
4. Equal treatment and pay for Peninsular (Spaniards born in Spain) and Insular (those born in the Philippines) civil servants.
5. Abolition of the power of the government to banish civil citizens.
6. Legal equality of all persons.

Aguinaldo established the Republika ng Pilipinas (Republic of the Philippines) on November 1, 1897, with himself as president.[1] However, Aguinaldo's government was unsuccessful in securing any international recognition of their presumptive new state. Shortly afterwards, on December 14, 1897, Aguinaldo and his top officials signed the Pact of Biak-na-Bato, which dissolved the brand-new Republic of the Philippines on the grounds that Aguinaldo and his officers would be paid 200,000 pesos collectively to exile

Flag of the late 1897 revolutionary republic of the Philippines, known by historians as the Republic of Biak-na-Bato. This government received no foreign recognition and was dissolved by Aguinaldo on December 14, 1897, six weeks after its founding, as part of a deal with the ruling Manila government. (Artemio Ricarte, CC BY-SA 4.0 https://creativecommons.org/licenses/by-sa/4.0, via Wikimedia Commons)

---

[1] Modern historians refer to this brief state as the Republika ng Biak-na-Bato (Republic of Biak-na-Bato) to avoid confusion with the current Republic of the Philippines.

A 1919 map of the 1898 Spanish–American War, displaying the main theaters of conflict around the world. Guam, Puerto Rico, Cuba, the Philippines, Manila Bay, and Santiago harbor are all represented, although not to scale with each other. (LOC Geography and Map Division)

themselves to Hong Kong while the Manila government attempted to institute reforms free of revolutionary violence. The Pact asserted that if the Manila government failed to reform, the exiles were free to return to the Philippines. The Pact temporarily reduced hostilities but never eliminated them.

THE CUBAN CRISIS, 1898

Since the US annexation of Florida in 1819, the United States mainland lay just 90nm from Spanish-controlled Cuba. Many Americans believed Cuba was a natural territory for US expansion. Several serious US schemes to purchase or annex Cuba were proposed throughout the 19th century, but all failed. Additionally, American sympathy ran high for Cuba's indigenous population, which was heavily oppressed by the ruling Spanish government.

In 1868, Cuba erupted in a vicious ten-year rebellion, which in 1873 nearly dragged the wholly unprepared United States into war with Spain before Spanish authority was fully re-established in 1878. However, in 1895, a second major revolt broke out in eastern Cuba. By January 1896, some 80,000 Spanish troops had arrived to suppress the increasingly ruthless insurrection. Engaging in scorched earth tactics, the rebels hoped to force the hand of the US government, as there was as much as $50 million of American money invested in the Cuban economy. However, Spanish authorities now resorted to the equally ruthless *reconcentrado* strategy of systematically herding rural Cubans into concentration camps. Although militarily effective, this caused enormous suffering and generated great anti-Spanish feeling throughout the United States.

Late on February 15, 1898, US battleship *Maine*, on a diplomatic visit to Havana, capital of Cuba, suddenly exploded, killing 268 of 367 men aboard. By March 9, rising anti-Spanish sentiment convinced the US Congress to unanimously authorize $50 million for defense.

On March 21, a USN board of inquiry concluded that *Maine* had most likely been destroyed by an external explosion – that is, by a third party – but refused to suggest who might have done it. Eight days later, on March 29, the US government issued what was effectively an ultimatum to Spain to evacuate Cuba immediately, which Madrid refused out of hand.

On April 19, 1898, the US Congress passed a joint resolution to recognize Cuba's independence from Spain and authorizing President McKinley to "use the land and naval forces to carry these resolutions into effect." Seizing the moral high ground, Congress belatedly attached the high-minded "Teller Amendment" to the ultimatum that foreswore any postwar US annexation of Cuba. On April 21, Spain broke off diplomatic relations with the United States. The USN commenced a blockade of Havana on April 22, and the following day, Spain declared war on the United States. The US government declared war on Spain on April 25. Although the war had erupted entirely over Cuba, somewhat to Spanish surprise the US government soon proved it was eager to strike Spanish outposts anywhere around the globe.

CHRONOLOGY

1896

August 26	Pro-independence Katipunan declares war against Manila government
December 30	Filipino nationalist José Rizal executed by Spanish authorities

1897

December 14	Pact of Biak-na-Bato signed, suspending Filipino revolution and authorizing 200,000 pesos to Aguinaldo and his cabinet to exile themselves

1898

February 15	Battleship USS *Maine* explodes in Havana harbor, Cuba
February 25	Roosevelt telegrams Dewey ordering the Asiatic Squadron to Hong Kong and to prepare for battle in the Philippines if war breaks out
March 9	US Congress passes "Fifty Million Dollar Bill" authorizing $50 million for national defense
March 29	US government issues Spain a virtual ultimatum regarding Cuba
April 19	US Congress passes joint resolution recognizing the independence of Cuba and authorizing the use of force to such end if necessary
April 21	Spanish government recalls ambassador and cuts diplomatic relations with the United States

April 22	President McKinley calls for 125,000 volunteers; USN begins naval blockade of Havana
April 23	Spanish government declares war on the United States
April 25	US Congress declares war on Spain
April 27	US Asiatic Squadron departs Mirs Bay for Manila Bay
May 1	US Asiatic Squadron crushes Spanish Escuadrón del Pacífico at battle of Manila Bay
May 2	Dewey requests reinforcements to conquer and control Manila
May 19	Aguinaldo returns to Philippines and reassumes control of Filipino revolution
May 25	First US troop convoy departs San Francisco for the Philippines
June 12	Aguinaldo issues Philippine Declaration of Independence
June 15	Second US troop convoy departs San Francisco for the Philippines
June 27	Third US troop convoy departs San Francisco for the Philippines
June 30	First US ground troops arrive in the Philippines
July 4	US Congress passes Newlands Resolution formally annexing the Republic of Hawai'i
July 15	Fourth US troop convoy departs San Francisco for the Philippines
July 29/30	US troops take over front-line insurgent trench south of Manila
July 31/August 1	"Battle in the Rain"
August 12	Global ceasefire signed between Spain and United States
August 13	Mock battle of Manila
December 10	Treaty of Paris signed, officially ending the Spanish–American War and transferring the Philippines to the United States

1899

February 4	War breaks out between United States and Philippine insurgents
February 6	US Congress ratifies Treaty of Paris annexing the Philippines to the United States

OPPOSING COMMANDERS

SPANISH

Spanish commanders during the 1898 war were almost categorical in their gloomy, fatalist approach to battle with the Americans, and even with the Filipinos. Spanish officers were handicapped by draconian Spanish law that made it a death penalty offense to surrender to an enemy without mounting a vigorous defense, no matter how suicidal the circumstances.

Governor-General of the Philippines Basilio Augustín y Dávila held that position from April 11 to July 24, 1898. Augustín is notable for attempting to make concessions to the Filipinos, and even allies out of them, in the sudden war against the Americans. However, such actions were far too little, too late, and largely backfired on Augustín. Once Augustín realized there would be no reinforcements to rescue Manila, his communiques became increasingly defeatist and hysterical. The Madrid government officially removed him as governor-general on July 24. Augustín allegedly slipped the US blockade in early August.

Governor-General of the Philippines Fermín Jáudenes y Álvarez was the last Spanish holder of that office, from August 4–13, 1898. He was promoted by Madrid to replace Augustín, who was in disgrace as a result of negotiating with the insurgents. By early August, Jáudenes realized he was in the same impossible situation as Augustín had been, and he engaged in secret negotiations with the Americans to surrender Manila to them instead of the insurgents.

The 58-year-old **Contraalmirante Patricio Montojo y Pasarón** commanded Spain's Escuadrón del Pacífico (Pacific Squadron) stationed in the Philippines. Montojo's first assignment to the Philippines was in 1860. As a newly minted sub-lieutenant, Montojo fought the Moros in Mindanao. Montojo was soon after promoted to lieutenant, and visited China and Cochinchina before returning to Spain in 1864. After tours and commands off Cuba and the River Plate, in the 1880s Montojo returned to the Philippines as a commodore, before returning to Spain in 1890.

Basilio Augustín y Dávila was governor-general of the Philippines for just six weeks, from April 11 to July 24, 1898. However, this encompassed most of the siege of Manila. During the insurgency, Augustín allowed his troops to be spread throughout Luzon, where they could be defeated in detail. (Naval History and Heritage Command, hereafter NHHC)

In September 1898, the Spanish government court-martialed Montojo for his defeat at Manila Bay and summoned the admiral to Spain. Despite favorable testimony from his old adversary, George Dewey, the Spanish government imprisoned Montojo in March 1899. Eventually Montojo was absolved, but he was ultimately discharged from the Armada. Montojo would die in Madrid on September 30, 1917.

The 63-year-old **Contraalmirante Manuel de la Cámara y Libermoore** commanded the cream of the remaining Armada Española (Spanish Navy), the Segundo Escuadrón (Second Squadron). Cámara was a deeply religious man who spoke fluent English thanks to his English mother. Cámara's orders were to "Avoid manifestly unfavorable encounters, considering as an essential point to avoid the useless sacrifice of the squadron and always to leave the honor of the troops without injury." These were shockingly different orders than those given to Montojo or to Montojo's counterpart, Cervera (dispatched to defend the West Indies). One must conclude that the Spanish government, safe in Madrid, had satisfied its own notion of honor once it had sacrificed Montojo's and Cervera's men on the altar of Old World gallantry. Instead, Cámara's mission was to save what territory or bargaining position for the Spanish government that he could in what would be the inevitably unfavorable peace negotiations to come.

Portrait of Contraalmirante Patricio Montojo y Pasarón, *circa* 1898. Montojo's outstanding feature was his humanitarianism. To Montojo, the idea of uselessly throwing away his men's lives in order to salvage the honor of the far-away Madrid government was abhorrent. Montojo's strategy at Manila Bay was to do his duty but save as many of his sailors as possible. (Public domain, via Wikimedia Commons)

AMERICAN

Republican **President William McKinley** was the US military's constitutional commander-in-chief. McKinley was the last American Civil War veteran to serve as president of the United States, having enlisted as a private and rising to major by 1865. The religious and hardworking McKinley was modest and sincere to a fault but lacked charisma or strong convictions. As president, McKinley was something of an empty suit – more valuable as an inoffensive figurehead than as a strong leader. Most alarmingly, McKinley possessed a "malleable" mind – he tended to trail events rather than drive them.

Secretary of the Navy John D. Long was a politician and attorney from Massachusetts. Long knew virtually nothing of naval affairs, providing a classic example of the American tradition of civilian control over the military. Long was moderate and conservative by nature. Yet despite the Roosevelt mythology, Long was fully in control of the Navy Department during the 1898 war.

Assistant Secretary of the Navy Theodore Roosevelt was described by a contemporary as "irrepressible, belligerent, and enthusiastic." The 39-year-old Roosevelt's strong personality imagined an aggressive Asiatic Squadron thrust into Manila Bay by his own hand-picked aggressive commander, and he ensured both transpired the way he wanted. Desperate to see battle himself, Roosevelt resigned as Assistant Secretary of the Navy on May 10, 1898 to raise a cavalry unit to fight in Cuba.

On January 3, 1898, 61-year-old **Commodore George Dewey** assumed command of the US Asiatic Squadron moored in Yokohama, Japan. He was at that time "a Commodore at the close of an honorable but obscure career." Dewey graduated fifth in the 1858 Annapolis class and as a junior officer had participated in numerous naval battles of the American Civil War. Although aggressive and energetic, the grandfatherly Dewey possessed a calm, unflappable persona that inspired his subordinates.

At the insistence of his personal friend Theodore Roosevelt, Dewey ultimately was appointed to the Asiatic Squadron command in October 1897, but without the usual promotion to rear admiral.

Dewey had immediately begun preparing for a possible war with Spain. He later wrote: "Farragut has always been my ideal of a naval officer, urbane, decisive, indomitable. Whenever I have been in a difficult situation, I have often asked myself, 'What would Farragut do?' I confess that I was thinking of him the night we entered Manila Bay, and with the conviction that I was doing precisely what he would have done. Valuable as the training of Annapolis was, it was poor schooling beside that of serving under Farragut in time of war."

For historians, Dewey is the most authoritative American source for the naval battle of Manila Bay, the overall Philippines campaign, and the history of wartime relations with the Filipino insurgents led by Emilio Aguinaldo. However, most of Dewey's written testimony came after the campaign, and particularly after the outbreak of the Philippine–American War, which erupted in 1899. Much of Dewey's later claims about his interactions with the Filipino insurgents in 1898 should therefore be taken carefully.

Captain Charles Vernon Gridley had assumed command of *Olympia* at Yokohama on July 29, 1897. The 53-year-old Gridley was an 1864 Annapolis graduate who had seen Civil War action under Farragut at Mobile Bay. By May 1898, Gridley was deathly ill with liver cancer. Due to his infirmity, he would be transferred home on May 25. However, by May 27 he would have to be transferred by stretcher from *Zafiro* to the merchantmen *Coptic*, observing, "I think I am done for it, personally." Just a few days later, on June 5, Gridley died aboard the *Coptic* in Kobe, Japan, never reaching home.

The US Army's First Philippine Expedition was commanded by 62-year-old **Brigadier-General Thomas M. Anderson**. Already a practicing attorney, Anderson had begun his army career in 1861, joining the 6th Ohio Volunteer Infantry as a private, but was commissioned a second lieutenant in the Regular Army on May 15, 1861. In 1897, Anderson was posted to Skagway, Alaska, during the Klondike Gold Rush. As the first US general to reach the Philippines on July 1, 1898, he became the inevitable second-in-command of the planned US ground forces.

President William McKinley, *circa* 1900. As a Republican, Ohioan, and Civil War veteran, McKinley ticked the necessary boxes for the period as a safe and inoffensive candidate. However, McKinley was notoriously indecisive and lacking in convictions. (LOC Prints and Photographs Division)

Commodore George Dewey leads his Asiatic Squadron into battle on May 1, 1898. Dewey famously stood on *Olympia*'s open flying bridge throughout the action. After Manila Bay, Dewey briefly became one of the most beloved celebrities in American popular culture history. (Courtesy of the Naval Historical Foundation, Collection of C. J. Dutreaux, NH 84510-KN)

Appointed to command the US Army's overall Philippine Expeditionary Force was 52-year-old **Major-General Wesley Merritt**. As an 1860 West Point graduate, Merritt was a career cavalryman who had fought in the American Civil War and the American Indian Wars. Merritt initially refused command of the Philippine Expeditionary Force unless it included regular troops instead of mere volunteers. This delayed Merritt's acceptance of command and his eventual arrival in the Philippines to July 25, 1898. Upon reaching the Philippines, Merritt reorganized the overall Philippine Expeditionary Force into the US Eighth Army Corps under his command. The Eighth Army Corps comprised a single division, the 2nd Division, whom Merritt assigned to Anderson.

During the war, Merritt never actually visited the US front lines. After the August 13 fall of Manila, Merritt became the first US military governor of the Philippines. He was then relieved on August 30 so that he could advise the US government during its Treaty of Paris negotiations. Although he knew nothing about the Philippines before he left the United States, Merritt correctly predicted to McKinley that "it seems more than probable we will have the insurgents to fight as well as the Spaniards."

Brigadier-General Francis Vinton Greene commanded the US Army's Second Philippine Expeditionary Force, which departed San Francisco on June 15 and arrived at Cavite on July 17. Greene would command the 2nd Brigade upon its establishment. **Brigadier-General Arthur MacArthur, Jr.** commanded the Third Philippine Expeditionary Force, which would arrive in the Philippines in early August and be the last US ground force to arrive before the official end of the war.

FILIPINO

The revolutionary Katipunan functioned as a sort of shadow government to the Madrid-backed state operating out of Manila. The Katipunan had a Supreme President, Comptroller, Fiscal (officer), Secretary of State, Secretary of War, Secretary of Justice, Secretary of Interior, Secretary of

Finance, Treasurer, and Financier. At the outbreak of war in 1896, the Katipunan was further reorganized into a cabinet, which the Katipunan regarded as a genuine wartime revolutionary government. In each Filipino province, the Katipunan established a *Sangguniang Bayan* (provincial council), and in each town put in place an organized popular council called the *Sangguniang Balangay*. Each Bayan and Balangay elected its own set of officials.

In 1898, upon hearing that Cuba was to be granted independence, Dewey wired from Manila: "These people are far superior in their intelligence, and more capable of self-government than the people of Cuba, and I am familiar with both races."

The Katipunan's army was the Philippine Revolutionary Army, or Panghimagsikang Hukbong Katihan ng Pilipinas in Tagalog. The Revolutionary Army had aspirations of being a formal army for a formal state, and thus based much of its organization and regulations on the regular Spanish Army's 1896 Ordenanza del Ejércitos.

The unquestioned military and political leader of the Philippine insurrection was 29-year-old **Generalissimo Emilio Aguinaldo y Famy**, a man of extraordinary intelligence, energy, and charisma. Despite being a schoolteacher of mixed Filipino and Chinese ancestry possessing no formal military training, it was Aguinaldo who almost singlehandedly transformed the Filipino Revolutionary Army into a formidable battlefield opponent.

Contemporary historian James H. Blount observed that Aguinaldo "was insignificant looking physically... but his presence suggested a high order of intelligence and a baffling reserve." A US major-general later summed Aguinaldo up as "Honest, sincere, and a natural leader of men." According to US General Funston in 1901, "He is a man of many excellent qualities and far and away the best Filipino I was ever brought in contact with."

In addition to proving himself a talented military leader, the incorruptible Aguinaldo was a true idealist, who time and again refused to be bought off by his enemies or his supposed allies. Virtually alone among the insurgent commanders, Aguinaldo consistently displayed an extraordinary magnanimity towards both his Spanish enemies and his increasingly prevaricating American allies. While other Filipino generals might conceivably match Aguinaldo's military talent, it is impossible to imagine anyone else juggling the insurgency's difficult military and political demands with Aguinaldo's skill and tact.

General Mariano Noriel was the Malay commander of the "First Zone," the forward area of insurgents besieging Manila. In a matter of weeks, Noriel's men would completely defeat the Spanish garrisons in the Cavite district, taking 3,000 prisoners.

Major-General Wesley Merritt, the US Army's overall Philippine Expedition commander, in 1898. Merritt followed the instructions of his government but was notably wary of the high military effectiveness of the Filipino insurgents, and the likelihood of being forced to fight them soon after the Spanish. Merritt retired from the US Army in 1900 and died in 1910. (Mike Cline, public domain, via Wikimedia Commons)

OPPOSING FORCES

SPANISH

Spanish coast defenses at Manila Bay

Spanish coastal artillery was extensive. Although many Spanish guns were muzzle-loading, they were otherwise fully modern and dangerous pieces. The batteries listed below do not include an additional large number of wholly obsolete guns mounted around Manila Bay.

The entrance to Manila Bay was heavily fortified with coastal batteries. There were two batteries on the Bataan peninsula: Punta Gorda, with three 7in muzzle-loading rifles, and Punta Lassisi, with two 6.3in breech-loading rifles. Just off Bataan, the island of Corregidor wielded a single battery of three 8in muzzle-loading rifles, while the small isle of Caballo 2 miles south of Corregidor mounted three 5.9in breech-loading rifles. Another three 4.7in breech-loading rifled cannon were situated on the rock of El Fraile guarding the southern passage into Manila Bay. Finally, Punta Restinga, on Luzon 2½nm east–southeast of El Fraile had three 6.3in muzzle-loading rifles.

If the outer defenses were penetrated, there remained more coastal guns to deal with before reaching Manila. Off Cavite were two batteries: Sangley Point, with two 5.9in breech-loading rifles, and Cañacao, with one 4.7in breech-loading rifle.

Spanish naval mines at Manila Bay

In theory, Spanish naval mines should have been a major defensive asset at Manila Bay. However, the Philippines were poorly supported by naval mines, which were both too few in number and too poor in condition. There were 14 Mathieson-type British mines, but these were typically lacking electrical components such as wiring and fuses, and still awaiting installation. Additionally, the nitrocotton explosive was apparently in poor condition. Another 22 naval mines were improvised by installing explosives and torpedo detonators in existing buoys. These were deployed at Boca Raton, the entrance to Manila Bay. However, they were too few to effectively close the strait and ocean currents had pulled many out of place. Some mines were wired to a shore installation and manually detonated by an operator observing the scene.

Montojo knew his mine situation was badly deficient and had requested additional mines from Spain. These made it to Singapore by the time war was declared, upon which they were promptly impounded by the British.

Similarly, fresh nitroglycerin was requested from Hong Kong, but Montojo only received several miles of electrical cable.

The Armada Española

A few years earlier, *Olympia*'s Captain Gridley had opined, "So far as the discipline of the men and esprit de corps are concerned her navy compares with ours about as the Chinese navy compared with that of Japan during the recent wars." He added that Spanish sailors were poor, "not at all like they were two centuries ago." Indeed, Manila authorities had been required to conscript men into Montojo's squadron. The Armada owned several modern warships, but all were stationed in Spain.

A US soldier stands sentry by Spanish guns of the captured Cavite arsenal in 1898. Spanish defenses in the Manila Bay region were formidable on paper, but they would prove inadequate when subjected to the test of battle. (Donation of C. J. Dutreaux, NHHC USN 902951)

Montojo's Escuadrón del Pacífico

The seven major warships of Montojo's squadron combined for 11,000 tons displacement, barely half that of Dewey's ships, while mounting a combined 37 guns between 4.7in and 6.4in in size. Most were "unprotected" in that they lacked true armor. Montojo's warships were also in much poorer condition, and their combined 1,100 men significantly lower in morale and training than their American counterparts.

Montojo's flagship at the battle of Manila Bay was the iron-constructed, unprotected cruiser *Reina Cristina*, which been launched in 1887. *Reina Cristina* had a nominal battery of six 120mm (4.7in) guns, two 70mm Nordenfelt rapid-firing guns, three 57mm Nordenfelt rapid-firing guns, two 42mm Nordenfelt rapid-firing guns, and six 37mm guns. The cruiser also mounted three 350mm (13.7in) torpedo tubes. Top speed was nominally 16kts, but in reality closer to 10kts.

The 3,342-ton wooden-hulled unprotected cruiser *Castilla*, commissioned in 1882, exemplified the disastrous state of the Spanish naval defenses in the Philippines. *Castilla* nominally mounted four 150mm guns, two 120mm (4.7in) guns, six 57mm QF guns, and three 350mm torpedo tubes. However, *Castilla*'s men had been forced to employ concrete around its shaft to stop a serious leak. The result was that even *Castilla*'s obsolete powerplant was unusable, and it would have to be towed by *Reina Cristina* from Subic back to Cavite.

Velasco, *Don Antonio de Ulloa* and *Don Juan de Austria* were all Velasco-class unprotected cruisers displacing 1,152 tons. They each mounted a nominal four 6in guns, two 3in guns, two machine guns, and two 14in torpedo tubes. However, *Velasco* was out of action during the Manila Bay engagement, as its boilers had been removed for repair.

Isla de Luzón and *Isla de Cuba* were both Isla de Luzón-class second-class protected cruisers. Both displaced 1,030 tons and had been commissioned in 1887. They each mounted a nominal four 120mm/35 (4in) BL guns, four 57mm/43 (6-pdr) Nordenfelt guns, three 37mm/20 revolving guns, and three 356mm (14in) torpedo tubes.

General Lezo and *El Cano* were iron-hulled General Concha-class gunboats displacing 515 tons each. Both were commissioned in 1887 and mounted two 120mm guns and several smaller antipersonnel weapons. The 492-ton iron-hulled third-class gunboat *Marques del Duero* had been built in France in 1875. It mounted one 6.4in muzzle-loading rifle, two 4.7in breech-loaders, and machine guns. The 700-ton iron-hulled gunboat *Argos* was armed with a single 70mm gun, but would play little part in the battle. Montojo's 1,900-ton transport *Manila* mounted two small rapid-fire guns and had a crew of 77 men.

An Alfonso XII-class cruiser, either *Reina Cristina* or its sister *Reina Mercedes*, seen at anchor in the 1890s. The class was designed for colonial service and was unfit for combat against a first-class opponent. Neither *Reina Cristina* nor *Reina Mercedes* would survive the war. (U.S. Naval Historical Center Photograph. Courtesy of the U.S. Naval Academy, 1941, public domain, via Wikimedia Commons)

Cámara's Segundo Escuadrón

Cámara's Segundo Escuadrón at Cádiz in southern Spain contained the Armada's two truly powerful and dangerous warships: the 9,745-ton battleship *Pelayo* and the 9,235-ton armored cruiser *Emperador Carlos V*. In theory, both were fully modern, but in reality, they were both incomplete and rushed into service.

The 10,500-ton *Patriota* and 9,500-ton *Rapido* were former ocean liners that had been hastily purchased from Hamburg Amerika in April 1898 and armed as auxiliary cruisers. Destroyers *Audaz*, *Osado*, and *Proserpina* were all 400-ton Furor-class torpedo boat destroyers. Built in Scotland in 1897, they were among the most modern warships in the Armada Española and could make 27kts. Transports *Buenos Aires* and *Panay* would carry a combined 4,000 Spanish troops to help reverse the situation on land. Cámara's fleet was additionally accompanied by four colliers, each carrying 5,000 tons of coal.

Ejército del Tierra (Spanish Army)

Since 1808, the Spanish Army had forged a long and effective history in guerilla wars, both as the insurgent and the counterinsurgent. Spanish enlisted men were recruited from the peasantry and were hardy and tough, but the army was run by an aristocratic class more concerned with long-obsolete Old World notions rather than pragmatic military motives. Most telling, the Spanish Army was top-heavy, with one officer for every 5.3 men and one general for every 236 men.

When war erupted in April 1898, the Spanish Army numbered 350,000 troops (both regular and volunteer) deployed throughout the Spanish Empire. Only 100,000 troops were stationed in Spain, but some 200,000 were deployed to garrison and pacify Cuba, while 15,000 troops occupied Puerto Rico.

Spanish infantry engage in rifle drills on Manila's Luneta waterfront, sometime before the battle of Manila Bay. The average Spanish soldier was tough and loyal, but he was plagued by a bloated and inefficient officer class above him. (*Campaigning in the Philippines*, Karl Irving Faust, 1899)

As of October 1897, most of the Spanish Army's remaining 45,000 troops were deployed in the Philippines. However, by April 1898, desertion, disease, disbandment, and rotations back to Spain had reduced Spanish troop numbers in the Philippines to about 26,000. Of these, some 23,000 were stationed in Luzon, the Philippines' most important island, with 10,000–15,000 in the Manila/Cavite/Subic Bay capital region. The remaining 3,000 Spanish troops were scattered throughout the Philippines' southern islands.

Spanish infantry were armed with the bolt-action M1893 Mauser rifle, a fine weapon that fired a 7mm smokeless cartridge. However, some Spanish troops were still armed with license-built M1873 Remingtons, an obsolete weapon that fired a single-shot black powder .43 cartridge.

In addition to the 26,000 Spanish troops in the Philippines, there were about 17,000 indigenous Filipinos in militia units, but these generally melted away during the war, either deserting to the Americans or insurgents, or simply going home.

Spanish fortifications

Spanish outposts throughout the Philippines were fortified by the ubiquitous "blockhouse," which were all built to the same plan but often of different materials. They were 30ft square, two stories tall, built of stone, wood, or a combination of the two, and erected on high ground. Walls were fortified with cement or gravel, and loopholes allowed Spanish troops to fire while under cover. Blockhouses and other Spanish fortifications were typically guarded by trenches 6ft wide and 3ft deep, with earth thrown up another 5ft above the trench and covered with sandbags.

Manila/Intramuros fortifications

Manila lies at the mouth of the Pasig River and was well-situated for defense. To the south of the Pasig was the Intramuros, the fortified inner walled city of Old Manila that represented the heart of Spanish power in the Philippines.

The Intramuros' west wall had been designed to defend against an attack by sea; the south and east walls built to ward off an attack by land. The south wall was 3,300ft long, while the east wall was 1,600ft long, for a combined length of 4,900ft of wall to the south and east to defend against an attack by land. There were in fact two walls – an outer wall 15ft high and an inner wall 25ft high. Both walls were built of heavy masonry, about 15–20ft

Old Spanish guns at Fort Santiago, Manila, in 1898. Although many of Manila Bay's guns were muzzle-loaders rather than state-of-the-art breech-loaders, most of them were otherwise fairly modern. (NHHC NH 2366)

wide at their tops, and designed so that troops on the higher inner wall could fire down and over the heads of troops manning the outer wall. Outside the outer wall was a 100ft-wide moat, and between the inner and outer walls was another 125ft-wide moat. Inside the inner moat were three additional bastions connected to the inner wall by footbridges. All walls and bastions were surmounted by heavy artillery, both modern and ancient. However, both moats had been poorly maintained and were nearly filled with debris.

The Intramuros was supported by outlying defensive works, particularly to the south and east. The Intramuros' most critical location was the southwest corner, which lay just 1½nm from the coast and could be simultaneously assaulted by land and sea. The southern face of the Intramuros was therefore further protected by the 1584 Fort San Antonio Abad, which mounted a battery of 9.4in breech-loading rifles. In total, Manila was protected by 226 land-based guns, of which 164 were muzzle-loaders.

AMERICAN

US Navy
US naval forces were greatly influenced by the recent cultural and technological revolution of the "New Steel Navy." By 1898, the United States had built its navy from an international laughingstock just ten years earlier into one of the finest in the world in terms of technology, training, and morale. Its officers and men were well-paid, well-motivated, and knew their profession. However, the outdated reputation of the recently poor US Navy continued to hold sway in the minds of most Europeans. British contemporary H. W. Wilson later wrote that the Spanish Navy "was to a great extent a paper force, whereas the American Navy was generally under- rather than over-estimated, even in America… yet how enormous was its superiority to the Spanish Navy could not be altogether grasped, even by the Americans, without the actual test of battle."

Dewey's Asiatic Squadron
The great powers all kept their own naval presence in the Far East. However, the US Asiatic Squadron was unique in that its government did not possess a sovereign port in the Far East. The US Asiatic Squadron, having no true homeport, was forced to rely on the goodwill of other governments to purchase provisions and dry-dock time.

Dewey's preserved flagship Olympia *as moored in the Delaware River in Philadelphia.* Olympia *is one of the few ships from that era that has survived to the present day.* Olympia *was transferred into civilian hands in 1958. (R'lyeh Imaging from Philadelphia, USA, CC BY 2.0 https://creativecommons.org/licenses/by/2.0, via Wikimedia Commons)*

In 1896, the United States had only 18,000 tons of warships on station in China, compared to 23,000 tons for Germany, 28,000 tons for France, and nearly 60,000 tons each for Britain and Russia. The US cruisers usually alternated ports between Yokohama and Nagasaki in Japan, while gunboats both cruised the mainland Asia coast and plied the Yangtze, working upriver from Shanghai.

Dewey's Asiatic Squadron at the May 1, 1898 battle of Manila Bay comprised four US protected cruisers, two US gunboats, and a United States Revenue Service cutter, plus two accompanying supply ships. Not including the cutter and supply ships, Dewey's squadron of four cruisers and two gunboats combined for 19,000 tons displacement and some 53 guns of 5in to 8in caliber, plus 135 smaller guns.

All of Dewey's warships were of modern steel construction and mounted light to moderate levels of state-of-the-art armor protection in critical areas. The six warships were crewed by a combined 1,700 men of high training and morale. Top speed ranged between 11 and 21kts.

Dewey's flagship was his largest and most powerful warship, the 5,870-ton protected cruiser USS *Olympia*. Designed specifically for flagship service on the Asiatic station, *Olympia* was large for a contemporary protected cruiser and proved a near-perfect combination of speed, armor, and firepower. It was also new, having been commissioned barely three years earlier in 1895. *Olympia* mounted four 8in/35 BL rifles, ten 5in/40 rapid-firing guns, and 16 6-pdr guns.

Protected cruiser USS Baltimore *was the second-largest warship in Dewey's squadron after* Olympia. Baltimore's *skipper, Captain Nehemiah Dyer, was nicknamed "Snarlyowl" by the crew. One anecdote held that Dyer had once thrown an objectionable apprentice boy out of the ship through a porthole. (Edward Hart, Detroit Publishing Co., LOC)*

Protected cruiser USS *Boston* steaming off San Francisco, *circa* 1892–93. Although undersized and obsolescent when built, *Boston* was one of the "ABC" trio of small cruisers that is regarded as the beginning of the United States' "Steel Navy" revolution. (NHHC NH 73387 via Navsource)

The second largest and most powerful warship in Dewey's command was the 4,600-ton protected cruiser USS *Baltimore*, commissioned in 1890. *Baltimore* mounted four 8in/35 guns, six 6in/30 guns, four 6-pdrs, and a battery of antipersonnel weapons.

The 3,200-ton protected cruiser USS *Raleigh* had been commissioned in 1894. *Raleigh* mounted one 6in gun, ten 5in guns, and eight 6-pdrs. Commissioned in 1887, the 3,200-ton protected cruiser USS *Boston* was the oldest and least modern warship in Dewey's squadron, but nevertheless mounted two 8in guns, six 6in guns, two 6-pdrs, and the usual handful of antipersonnel weapons.

The 1,710-ton gunboat USS *Concord*, commissioned in 1891, mounted six 6in/30 guns and had a top speed of 16kts. The small 867-ton gunboat USS *Petrel* had been commissioned in 1889 and had a top speed 11.5kts. Mounting 6in guns, *Petrel* was nicknamed the "Baby Battleship."

A United States Revenue Service cutter, USRC *McCulloch*, had been commissioned on December 12, 1897 on the US East Coast. En route to San Francisco via the Suez Canal, it was ordered to Dewey's Asiatic Squadron as reinforcement. The 1,280-ton *McCulloch* mounted four 3in guns and a bow torpedo tube.

Supporting Dewey's squadron at sea were two purchased colliers. The first, *Nanshan*, was built in 1896 and displaced 5,059 tons. The second collier, *Zafiro*, was built in 1884. Both *Nanshan* and *Zafiro* had civilian crews of roughly 45 men each.

Left behind in Shanghai was Dewey's ancient and decrepit gunboat USS *Monocacy*, an obsolete relic long unfit for battle on the high seas. However, a third of *Monocacy*'s men and half its officers were ordered to Hong Kong to join Dewey's squadron.

Asiatic Squadron reinforcements

Commissioned in 1889, the 4,040-ton protected cruiser USS *Charleston* was stationed at San Francisco in early 1898 as part of the Pacific Squadron. *Charleston* mounted two 8in/35 guns, six 6in/30 guns, four 6-pdrs, and a battery of antipersonnel guns.

Ancient harbor defense monitors USS *Monterey* and USS *Monadnock* were also stationed in San Francisco. Although slow, ugly, and ungainly, they were armed with two double turrets of 10in to 12in battleship guns and were fully protected by battleship armor. However, their sea keeping was so poor that the only way they could reach the Philippines was if they were towed across the entire Pacific. But if the monitors arrived in time, they would provide Dewey with truly powerful assets to counter any enemy battleship.

Additionally, the captured Spanish gunboats *Pampanga*, *Paragua*, and *Callao* would all be commissioned into USN service in 1898 and would provide valuable support during the unfolding Philippines campaign.

US Navy forces in the Atlantic

Most of the US Navy was stationed in the Atlantic. Significant US warships not directly available for the 1898 Philippines campaign were the battleships *Texas*, *Indiana*, *Massachusetts*, *Oregon*, and *Iowa*, armored cruisers *New York* and *Brooklyn*, and numerous protected cruisers, gunboats, armed yachts, and monitors. However, the very existence of these ships in the Atlantic would directly affect US success in the Philippines by providing a dangerous fleet-in-being available for use against the Spanish homeland.

US Army

By now, the American Civil War was more than a generation in the past. According to a US brigadier-general, by 1898, "Only the poetry and fiction of war existed; the actual privations and hardships of war our young men knew nothing about."

The late 1890s US Army was essentially a small constabulary force that had been heavily influenced by the Indian Wars of the American frontier. The prewar Regular Army comprised about 28,000 men in total, dispersed around the United States in 78 individual posts; its largest single garrison comprised barely 850 men. Indeed, the Regular Army was considerably smaller than Mexico's army, and just one-twentieth the size of Germany's.

Mobilization plans against a major power derived from American Civil War experience, in which the tiny professional Regular Army would both recruit vast numbers of new, raw volunteers as well as absorbing the organized state militias into its command structure. In early 1898, these state militias combined for a manpower of 115,627.

Inspired by Lincoln's 1861 call-up, on April 22, 1898, President McKinley called for 125,000 volunteers. This proved a gross overestimation of what was needed or even useful. By August 1, 1898, total US Army strength was 272,046, even though only 50,000 ever deployed overseas. Despite the vast increase in US Army size, only 471 officers and 10,432 enlisted men of the US Eighth Army Corps would reach Manila by the city's fall on August 13, 1898.

By 1898, most Regular (federal) infantry were armed with the bolt-action .30-40 Krag-Jörgensen rifle or carbine. However, some Regular and most state infantry still used the obsolete M1873 .45-70 Springfield rifle or carbine, which were single-shot and used smoky black powder cartridges.

Battery D of the 6th US Artillery at Manila in 1898. Despite the hurried and ad hoc nature of the Philippine Expedition, the Americans successfully transported a combined-arms force to the Manila region, including the only modern field artillery brought to bear against the Spaniards. (NHHC WHI.2014.64)

FILIPINO

The official military of the First Philippine Republic was the Philippine Revolutionary Army (or Panghimagsikang Hukbong Katihan ng Pilipinas). It had been established in March 1897 and would be dissolved in

December 1899. In some ways, its ideological organization surprised the Americans, as Aguinaldo promulgated considerable legal paperwork and regulations to run the army as would befit any Western military. However, the Philippine Revolutionary Army's insistence on fighting Western armies in the conventional Western fashion, instead of employing more appropriate guerilla tactics, would prove an Achilles heel throughout its existence.

Although surprisingly effective and disciplined, the Filipino insurgent army was loosely organized by province. Each province was led by a commanding general, who was compelled to maintain companies of insurgents, based on population. Usually, four companies together combined into a battalion.

Oscar F. Williams, US Consul in the Philippines, held the prevailing early view of the Filipino insurgents, which he claimed were "brave, submissive, and cheaply provided for" and would "cheerfully follow [the American] flag" in a decisive attack on Manila. However, contemporary historian James H. Blount observed: "Our ablest [American officers] in the early days were the first to cease considering the little brown soldiers a joke, and their government an *opera-bouffe* affair."

The fluid nature of the Filipino insurgency means the exact number of Filipino troops at any given time and place is difficult to ascertain. However, by July 8, 1898, Aguinaldo had assumed direct command of an army of 15,000 Filipino fighting men, including 11,000 with guns. By early August, Filipino insurgent strength was about 30,000 men, with 20,000 in Luzon.

According to contemporary historian Frank D. Millett:

> It was an interesting sight to see the insurgents strolling to and from the front. Pretty much all day long they were coming and going, never in military formation, but singly, and in small groups, perfectly clean and tidy in dress, often accompanied by their wives and children, and all chatting as merrily as if they were going off on a pigeon shoot. The men who sold fish and vegetables in camp in the morning would be seen every day or two dressed in holiday garments, with rifle and cartridge boxes, strolling off to take their turn at the Spaniards.

There were many more Filipino insurgents than there were available rifles. Those not armed with rifles often sported a bolo, the native sword. An insurgent typically served 24 hours on the front line, then returned home for a rest, passing his weaponry to his arriving replacement: "thus a limited number of weapons served to arm a great many besiegers." Many were former volunteer militia. The insurgents "were perfectly obedient to orders... and made the most devoted soldiers."

Although insurgent soldiers in the Philippine Revolutionary Army lacked a formal logistic system, food was plentiful and brought to within 200 yards of the trenches and cooked by Filipino women. A typical ration was a double handful of rice "sometimes enriched by a small proportion of meat or fish" and served in a plantain leaf. An American observer noted the Filipinos "did not seem bothered by thirst like our men." (US Army Signal Corps, public domain, via Wikimedia Commons)

ORDERS OF BATTLE

KINGDOM OF SPAIN

ARMADA ESPAÑOLA

Escuadrón del Pacífico (Manila) – Contraalmirante Patricio Montojo y Pasarón
Unprotected cruiser *Reina Cristina* (Montojo)
Unprotected cruiser *Castilla*
Protected cruiser *Isla de Cuba*
Protected cruiser *Isla de Luzón*
Unprotected cruiser *Don Antonio de Ulloa*
Unprotected cruiser *Don Juan de Austria*
Gunboat *Marques del Duero*
Gunboat *General Lezo*
Unprotected cruiser *Velasco*
Gunboat *El Cano*
Gunboat *Argos*
Transport *Manila*
More than 20 additional small Spanish gunboats operated throughout the Philippines: *Quiros, Villalobos, Maniteno, Mariveles, Mindoro, Panay, Albay, Calamianes, Leyte, Arayat, Balusan, Callao, Pampanga, Paragua, Samar, Basco, Gardoqui, Otalora, Barcelo, Urdaneta, Cebu, General Alava*

Segundo Escuadrón (Cádiz) – Contraalmirante Manuel de la Cámara
Battleship *Pelayo* (Cámara)
Armored cruiser *Emperador Carlos V*
Auxiliary cruiser *Patriota*
Auxiliary cruiser *Rapido*
Destroyer *Audaz*
Destroyer *Osado*
Destroyer *Proserpina*
Transport *Buenos Aires*
Transport *Panay*

EJÉRCITO ESPAÑOL IN THE PHILIPPINES (OCTOBER 1897)

Military District of Luzon
1º Batallón Expedicionario de Fusileros
2º Batallón Expedicionario de Fusileros
3º Batallón Expedicionario de Fusileros
4º Batallón Expedicionario de Fusileros
5º Batallón Expedicionario de Fusileros
6º Batallón Expedicionario de Fusileros
7º Batallón Expedicionario de Fusileros
8º Batallón Expedicionario de Fusileros
9º Batallón Expedicionario de Fusileros
10º Batallón Expedicionario de Fusileros
11º Batallón Expedicionario de Fusileros
12º Batallón Expedicionario de Fusileros
13º Batallón Expedicionario de Fusileros
14º Batallón Expedicionario de Fusileros
15º Batallón Expedicionario de Fusileros
1º Regimiento de Infantería de Marina
31º Regimiento de Caballería de Filipinas
Regimiento de la Plaza (fortress artillery)
6º Regimiento de Artillería (mountain artillery)
1º Escuadrón Expedicionario de Lancero (lancers)
Batallón de ingenieros (engineers)
Batallón de Carabineros (volunteer riflemen)
Brigada de transporte

Guardia Civil Regiments
Regimiento de la Guardia Civil Nº 20
Regimiento de la Guardia Civil Nº 21
Regimiento de la Guardia Civil Nº 22

Native regiments
Regimiento Nativo Nº 68 (Legaspi) (2x battalions)
Regimiento Nativo Nº 69 (Iberia) (2x battalions)
Regimiento Nativo Nº 70 (Magallanes) (1x battalion)
Regimiento Nativo Nº 71 (Mindanao) (2x battalions)
Regimiento Nativo Nº 72 (Visayas) (1x battalion)
Regimiento Nativo Nº 73 (Jolo) (2x battalions)
Regimiento Nativo Nº 74 (Manila) (2x battalions)

UNITED STATES

UNITED STATES NAVY

Asiatic Squadron (Hong Kong) – Commodore George Dewey
Protected cruiser USS *Olympia* (Dewey)
Protected cruiser USS *Baltimore*
Protected cruiser USS *Raleigh*
Protected cruiser USS *Boston*
Gunboat USS *Concord*
Gunboat USS *Petrel*
Cutter USRC *McCulloch*
Collier *Nanshan*
Collier *Zafiro*
Gunboat USS *Monocacy* (laid up in Shanghai)

Pacific Squadron (San Francisco) reinforcements
Protected cruiser USS *Charleston*
Monitor USS *Monterey*
Monitor USS *Monadnock*

First Philippine Expedition – Brigadier-General Thomas M. Anderson
Transports *Australia, City of Sydney, City of Peking*

Second Philippine Expedition – Brigadier-General Francis V. Greene
Transports *China, Senator, Zealandia, Colon*

Third Philippine Expedition – Brigadier-General Arthur MacArthur, Jr.
Transports *Newport, Indiana, Morgan City, Ohio, Valencia, City of Para*

UNITED STATES ARMY PHILIPPINES EXPEDITION

US Eighth Army Corps – Major-General Wesley Merritt
US 2nd Division – Brigadier-General Thomas M. Anderson
1st Brigade – Brigadier-General Arthur MacArthur, Jr.
    23rd US Infantry – Colonel John W. French
    14th US Infantry
    13th Minnesota Volunteer Infantry
    1st North Dakota Volunteer Infantry
    1st Idaho Volunteer Infantry
    1st Wyoming Volunteer Infantry
    Astor Battery
2nd Brigade – Brigadier-General Francis V. Greene
    18th US Infantry, 1st Battalion – Colonel C. M. Bailey
    18th US Infantry, 2nd Battalion – Major Charles Kellar
    3rd US Artillery, 1st Battalion – Captain James O'Hara
    3rd US Artillery, 2nd Battalion – Captain W. E. Birkhimer
    US Engineers, Company A – Second Lieutenant William D. Connor
    1st California Volunteer Infantry – Colonel James S. Smith
    1st Colorado Volunteer Infantry – Colonel Irving Hale
    1st Nebraska Volunteer Infantry – Colonel John P. Bratt
    10th Pennsylvania Volunteer Infantry – Colonel A. L. Hawkins
    Utah Volunteer Artillery, Light Battery A – Captain R. W. Young
    Utah Volunteer Artillery, Light Battery B – Captain F. A. Grant
    2nd Oregon Volunteer Infantry
    California Volunteer Heavy Artillery Detachment

OPPOSING PLANS

SPANISH

The Spanish government was under no illusions. As early as 1895, the governor-general of Cuba had observed that in a potential war with the United States, "honor is more important than success." Madrid assumed Cuba had no chance of surviving the US onslaught, but it initially believed the Philippines could be retained against the insurrection.

On April 23, 1898, the Spanish naval high command in Madrid ordered its major fleet units to concentrate at Cádiz. This force was designated the Segundo Escuadrón and was put under the command of Contraalmirante Manuel de la Cámara y Libermoore.

The Spaniards' primary goals in the Philippines were to defend the archipelago as a final outpost of the Spanish Empire; to salvage Spanish honor by fighting gallantly; and, as far as Montojo was concerned, to allow as many men as possible of the seemingly doomed Escuadrón del Pacífico to survive the battle. No Spanish officer truly believed their overmatched flotilla could defeat the descending US Asiatic Squadron. Indeed, for all of the tense nervousness within the American force, and the arrogance of observing European powers, in the end only the Spaniards had correctly divined the near-certain course of events.

On land, Governor-General Augustín would foolishly attempt to defend all of Luzon, spreading his troops out and then pinning them to small, fixed garrisons instead of immediately concentrating them in fortified Manila. Although probably outnumbered overall, the Filipino insurgents stayed massed and repeatedly defeated Spanish outposts in detail, proving Frederick's military maxim that "He who defends everything defends nothing."

AMERICAN

Official US planning for a war with Spain had started in 1894, beginning with Lieutenant Commander Charles J. Train's paper "Strategy in the Event of War with Spain."

The Office of Naval Intelligence's Lieutenant William Kimball's subsequent 1896 plan included an attack on Manila Bay. However, the Naval War College (NWC) criticized Kimball's plan for several reasons: it dissipated US naval strength to dangerous levels; a successful blockade of

Cuba was assumed impossible; and a bombardment of Spain might harden Spanish resolve and invite European intervention. However, the NWC president, Captain Henry Taylor, endorsed one aspect of Kimball's plan – the descent of the Asiatic Squadron on Manila Bay.

In summer 1896, Rear Admiral Francis Ramsey conducted another study. The Ramsey board also urged a tight Cuba blockade, but added Puerto Rico. Ravaged by war, the starving Cubans and Puerto Ricans would be unable to feed themselves, and an augmented US fleet would intercept and destroy any relief convoy from Europe. Furthermore, the US Atlantic Fleet, reinforced by the Asiatic Squadron, would capture the Canary Islands as an advanced base to operate directly against the Spanish homeland.

In June 1897, incoming Secretary of the Navy Long ordered a third study. The resulting Sicard board returned to a joint operation against Havana requiring a close and augmented blockade and abandoned a descent on the Canaries, but suggested a "flying squadron" of two armored cruisers and two commerce destroyers to harass Spanish shipping off Spain. The Sicard plan also resurrected Kimball's idea of using the Asiatic Squadron to descend on the Philippines.

However, any strike against the Philippines portended obvious logistic problems. International law required belligerent warships to immediately depart all neutral ports or risk internment of the ships and crews. This caused a grave problem for the US Asiatic Squadron, whose nearest friendly port was Honolulu and nearest sovereign port was San Francisco.

Ironically, before Dewey's unexpected and smashing victory, there is zero evidence that the US government or American people had imperial designs on the Philippines. There was simply a Spanish squadron there, so the US government attacked it. Indeed, even after Manila Bay, Washington's political guidance regarding the campaign was vague to non-existent. On May 2, Major-General Merritt, still in the United States, requested a clarification of US objectives in the Philippines. McKinley finally responded on May 19 with the vague claim that the United States' "two-fold purpose" comprised "the reduction of Spanish power in that quarter" followed by the introduction of "order and security of the islands while in the possession of the United States." The circumstances, character, and duration of such American "possession" were not addressed. Such was the extent of Dewey's and Merritt's direction from Washington.

An 1890s view of the Naval War College in Newport, Rhode Island. The main building seen here faces Narragansett Bay and is now known as Luce Hall. It is here that much of the prewar planning against Spain was done in the mid-1890s. (NHHC)

One last factor deserves mention. While the United States had no official allies in the 1898 war, the Americans did receive important if indirect support from the officially neutral British government. As the world's premiere global empire, it was simply in British geopolitical interests that no existing European power profit off the Spanish Empire's corpse.

FILIPINO

By 1898, Filipino plans were intended to force a political revolution that would result in complete independence from Spain or any other foreign power. This would be achieved militarily by the wearing down of Spanish forces with numbers and attrition, as well as – initially – enthusiastically embracing the Americans as political and operational allies.

The December 1897 Pact of Biak-na-Bato had been a complex and cynical agreement between the Spanish government and the Filipino revolutionaries to end or at least suspend the destructive and seemingly indecisive Philippine Revolution. Under the terms of Biak-na-Bato, the Spanish government promised that the Filipinos would have the right to be represented in the Spanish Cortes, that the friars would be reduced in power, and that Aguinaldo and his cabinet would be paid 200,000 Mexican pesos if they would voluntarily exile themselves overseas. No definite time was fixed, and if Spanish promises went unfulfilled, Aguinaldo and his men would have the right to return to the Philippines. Aguinaldo agreed to surrender the rebel arms and fortifications, to disband the insurgent army, and to council submission to Spanish authority while the promised Spanish reforms were underway.

On January 2, 1898, thinking they had bought off Aguinaldo, the Spanish government paid the 200,000 pesos upon Aguinaldo's arrival in Hong Kong. However, Aguinaldo immediately invested the Spanish indemnity not into personal luxuries but into buying weapons and other war materiel needed for an inevitable return to the Philippines. The Spanish had not bought off Aguinaldo as they had planned; they had simply armed him.

Barely two months into Aguinaldo's exile, the *Maine* blew up and a war between Spain and the "Great North American Republic" looked increasingly likely. Almost simultaneously, it became apparent that the Spanish government had no intentions of honoring its Biak-na-Bato agreement to institute reforms. On March 25, 1898, Manila police suddenly attacked a group of Visayan sailors accused of publicly seditious talk, shooting 70 of them. By April 3, an army of 5,000 Visayan insurgents captured most of the city of Cebu. Reinforcements from Manila drove out the insurgents, while another large battle took place at Labangan, killing 1,000 insurgents.

Luzon now erupted back into rebellion; Faust reported that "In the provinces north of and adjoining Manila, the looting and killing was like that of savages." A force of 1,000 Spaniards under General Ricardo Monet was sent to quell the revolt but proved incapable of doing so.

Secretary of the Navy John D. Long seen in an 1897 portrait. A mild-mannered Massachusetts Republican, Long tends to be overshadowed by his deputy, Theodore Roosevelt. However, Long was fully in control of the Navy Department. Long resigned as Secretary in 1901 after his former assistant became president. (LOC Prints and Photographs Division)

The Filipino negotiators for the Pact of Biak-na-Bato. Seated in front are Pedro Paterno on the left and Emilio Aguinaldo on the right. General Llanera is standing at the back on the right. The Americans observed that Filipinos were especially fond of "paperwork," with Blount stating that Filipino *escribientes* "can work like bees in drafting documents." (Public domain, via Wikimedia Commons)

On April 21, Aguinaldo met US Consul-General Spencer Pratt in Singapore. Pratt convinced Aguinaldo to collaborate with the Americans, implying the US had no interest in the Philippines. According to Aguinaldo, together they drew up a draft agreement between the Filipino insurgents and the United States. Among its many provisions were Filipino independence from Spain; a temporary American and European administrative commission over the Philippines; a Cuba-style American protectorate over the Philippines; free international trade; judicial reform; freedom of speech, press, and religion; the expulsion of the corrupt monastic order; a vigorous program to build Filipino infrastructure; and the prevention of reprisals against Spaniards.

Aguinaldo knew any draft treaty held zero power until it was ratified by the US government, which he certainly expected would be the case. However, in later testimony, Pratt denied making any promises to Aguinaldo, and further claimed that he stressed to Aguinaldo that he did not have the authority to make the promises Aguinaldo desired.

Aguinaldo, still in Singapore with Pratt, but wishing to rejoin the war alongside the Americans, now requested a written statement from Dewey in Hong Kong that the United States would guarantee Filipino independence under Aguinaldo's leadership. Dewey merely telegraphed, "Tell Aguinaldo come soon as possible." A suspicious Aguinaldo queried Pratt, who claimed that Dewey had privately assured Pratt that the US government would "at least recognize Filipino independence under an American naval protectorate."

However, the current insurgency against the Manila government had been fought with a particular barbarity, and US government officials did not believe either US or Filipino officers could prevent violent reprisals against defeated Spaniards. The US government, not wanting to be held responsible in the eyes of the world for the expected Filipino atrocities against captured Spanish citizens, thus refused to publicly recognize Aguinaldo's government in any capacity.

According to historian Albert A. Nofi: "Charges of mendacity and conspiracy fly freely in discussions of these negotiations, but the most likely explanation is that neither side knew precisely what it wanted from the other, and both heard what they wanted to hear."

The Philippines, 1898

THE CAMPAIGN

PRELUDE

The *Maine* disaster had virtually ensured the long-simmering Spanish–American tensions would finally resolve with war. Strategic preparations were necessary; no time was wasted waiting for the report of the official investigation into the sinking.

On January 27, the Navy Department cabled Dewey: "Retain until further orders the crew of the squadron whose terms of enlistment have expired."

On February 9, the gunboat USS *Concord* arrived in Yokohama from Honolulu with 35 tons of ammunition for the Asiatic Squadron. *Concord* transferred its ammunition to *Olympia* the following day, and on February 11, *Olympia* departed Yokohama for Hong Kong, where it would rendezvous with the gunboat *Petrel* en route to Canton to show the flag during Chinese New Year festivities. *Olympia* reached Hong Kong on February 17, where the crew suddenly learned of the *Maine* disaster. On February 25, a telegram from Roosevelt commanded Dewey: "Order the squadron, except *Monocacy*, to Hong Kong. Keep full of coal. In the event declaration of war Spain, your duty will be to see that the Spanish squadron does not leave the Asiatic coast, and then offensive operations in Philippine Islands. Keep *Olympia* until further orders."

Olympia, Dewey's flagship, had been due to rotate back home for refit. But for the most powerful US warship in the Far East to miss the impending Pacific naval war with Spain was unthinkable. Dewey would instead receive *Olympia*'s intended replacement, the cruiser *Baltimore*, and also retain *Olympia* for the duration of hostilities. For its part, *Baltimore*, the current US Pacific Squadron flagship, remained at its homeport of Honolulu until it could pick up a shipment of ammunition en route from the West Coast to help augment Dewey's Asiatic Squadron.

Dewey boards *Olympia* in 1898. Dewey's appointment as Asiatic Squadron commander was personally pushed through by Roosevelt, who must have recognized something of his own unflappable aggressiveness in the otherwise placid-looking Dewey. (Photograph by George Grantham, NHHC NH 43379)

Olympia delivering a gun salute at Hong Kong in February 1898, possibly for George Washington's birthday. Naval gunnery was just a few years away from a technological revolution, but American gunnery in 1898 was probably as good as any navy's and certainly proved better than Spain's. (Courtesy of the Naval Historical Foundation, Dutreaux Collection, NHHC NH 84574)

Weeks earlier, Dewey had discovered the Far East's best coal had already been purchased by other nations' vessels. The US government accordingly purchased coal from Cardiff in Wales, widely agreed to be the best in the world, and had it shipped to Dewey aboard the colliers *Nanshan* and *Zafiro*. When *Nanshan* arrived at Hong Kong on April 6, Dewey received permission from the US government to purchase *Nanshan* outright for the sum of $155,728. *Zafiro* arrived at Hong Kong three days later, on April 9, and was likewise purchased by the US government, this time from the China & Manila Steamship Company for $87,597. Secretary Long ordered Dewey to arm the colliers, but Dewey wisely disobeyed – so long as the merchantmen were unarmed they were noncombatants, and not subject to wartime neutrality laws. *Nanshan* and *Zafiro* could therefore legally enter any neutral port and purchase supplies. Dewey stationed one USN officer each aboard *Nanshan* and *Zafiro* to help coordinate movements; each USN officer was accompanied (unofficially) by several enlisted men to assist with signaling.

Desperate for intelligence, Dewey discovered that no US warship had visited Manila in 22 years, meaning there was no modern information on the bay's defenses. However, some intelligence was gleaned from interrogating commercial traffic. Meanwhile, despite death threats, the US Consul at Manila, Oscar Williams, doggedly stayed in Manila as long as possible and surreptitiously passed on as much information as possible to Dewey.

Weeks earlier, with war looming, Aguinaldo's Hong Kong exiles had lobbied to accompany Dewey's squadron to the Philippines. Dewey had first met some of Aguinaldo's officers (but not Aguinaldo himself) at Hong Kong around April 1, and later claimed that he was initially unimpressed: "They seemed to be all very young earnest boys. I did not attach much importance to what they said or to themselves… I was getting my squadron ready for battle, and these little men were coming on board my ship at Hong Kong and taking a good deal of my time."

On April 24, Secretary Long cabled Dewey at Hong Kong, announcing, "War has commenced between the United States and Spain. Proceed at once to Philippine Islands. Commence operations at once, particularly against Spanish fleet. You must capture vessels or destroy. Use utmost endeavors."

Simultaneously, Major-General Wilsone Black, the Acting Administrator of Hong Kong, reluctantly issued a proclamation of British neutrality. By international law, the US Asiatic Squadron had 24 hours to evacuate the port. Fortunately, *Baltimore* had arrived at Hong Kong the day before, suddenly becoming Dewey's second most powerful warship but also laden with its priceless cargo of ammunition. In a matter of hours, *Baltimore* had been quickly dry-docked at Hong Kong, its hull cleaned of fouling, and the white peacetime livery painted over with wartime gray.

Compelled by events, Dewey sortied the US Asiatic Squadron from Hong Kong to China's nearby Mirs Bay on April 25, and *Baltimore* immediately began doling out ammunition to the fleet. Hours later, Aguinaldo arrived back in Hong Kong from Singapore, having just missed the US squadron.

That same day, April 25, Montojo's Escuadrón del Pacífico departed Manila Bay. Montojo's destination was Subic Bay – Luzon's finest harbor, a deep, protected anchorage ringed by high mountains. However, after a conference at Subic the following morning, Montojo began to have doubts about confronting the Americans there.

Back at Mirs Bay, Dewey awaited US Consul Oscar Williams, who had recently fled Manila. Williams arrived at Mirs Bay on April 27, accompanied by Filipino insurgent Chief Alijandrini. Dewey and his officers convened a noon conference with Williams, who passed on all possible details of the Spanish forces' status and disposition.

At 1400hrs on April 27, the US Asiatic Squadron departed Mirs Bay and headed for the Philippines. Despite *Baltimore*'s efforts, Dewey knew his squadron would be going into battle with ammunition at only 60 percent capacity, with California the nearest source of reloads.

Back in Manila, Governor-General Augustín issued a general order of Special Military Service on April 23, essentially conscripting all males under the age of 50. In Madrid, the Archbishop issued a hyperbolic Proclamation to the Filipino People, lambasting the Americans and suddenly proclaiming the Filipinos to be brothers of the Spanish. The sudden about-face fooled no one. Manila was now under siege from both north and south by the Filipino insurgents. The capital erupted in chaos as any European or Chinese person with the means to do so fled the city. Among those who made the attempt were General Augustín's wife and children, who were captured by insurgents north of Manila. The handful of Americans hid among the foreign ships anchored in Manila Bay. On April 29, suspecting dubious loyalty among an indigenous militia regiment, Spanish authorities summarily executed six Filipino corporals. The following day, the entire Filipino regiment defected to the insurgents.

Also on April 29, Montojo abandoned Subic and headed back to Manila Bay. Montojo later gave several reasons for not making his stand at Subic. Four of the heavy guns intended to guard the mouth of Subic had not yet been installed and were six weeks behind schedule – although a US officer later claimed that all four guns were lying on the beach and could have been operational in 24 hours. Secondly, the badly leaking wooden-hulled *Castilla* was "merely a floating battery, incapable of maneuver." Additionally, the Spanish consul at Hong Kong had reported that Dewey was heading directly for Subic, which a council of Montojo's captains had claimed somehow made

Subic Bay as viewed in 1990. The deep water of the harbor is easily imagined by the dark blue water and high steep mountains ringing the port. Visible are the US Navy's Naval Air Station Cubi Point and Naval Station Subic Bay. (PH1[Nac] David R. Sanner, US Navy, public domain, via Wikimedia Commons)

Subic "unsupportable." Finally, Montojo concluded that the US squadron would certainly destroy all the Spanish warships, and that the Spanish crews would not be able to be saved because of Subic's 40m depth. The Americans were later shocked at this last notion, calling it "an amazing and unseamanlike notion," with even Dewey later exclaiming: "What a singular lack of morale... and what a strange conclusion for a naval officer!"

THE BATTLE OF MANILA BAY, MAY 1

Based on reports of the 1895–96 Sino-Japanese War, the Americans chose to "strip ship" and remove anything that might splinter or catch fire. Wooden furnishings were ripped out and thrown overboard, including pulpits and most mess tables. *Baltimore*'s Lieutenant Endicott observed the sea "strewn for fifty leagues with jettisoned woodwork."

Dewey's squadron, uncertain of Montojo's exact location, made landfall off Luzon's Cape Bolinao early on April 30. Dewey had hoped to face Montojo at Manila, but before leaving China Dewey had been told by Consul Williams that Montojo appeared to have steamed for Subic Bay. "Thus Admiral Montojo at the last moment seemed to have realized the strategic advantage of Subic over Manila, which we had hoped he would fail to do," Dewey later observed.

As the main squadron continued proceeding southwards at 8kts, Dewey dispatched *Boston* and *Concord* ahead to reconnoiter Subic Bay, expecting Montojo to be there. When US officers mistakenly believed they heard heavy guns firing, Dewey sent the heavier and more powerful *Baltimore* to support *Boston* and *Concord*, while *Olympia* and the rest of the squadron continued behind at 8kts, skirting the Luzon shoreline 3–4 miles away.

At 1530hrs, *Olympia* lookouts sighted Subic Bay and confirmed from *Baltimore*, *Boston*, and *Concord* that Subic was empty – Montojo could only be in Manila Bay. A relieved Dewey remarked to his chief-of-staff, "Now we have them." That afternoon, April 30, Dewey briefly assembled his captains aboard *Olympia* and explained his plan. Once they had returned to their ships, the squadron sortied for Manila Bay.

The squadron was in column, led by Dewey's flagship *Olympia*, followed by *Baltimore*, *Raleigh*, the gunboats *Petrel* and *Concord*, protected cruiser *Boston*, and revenue cutter *McCulloch*. The colliers *Zafiro* and *Nanshan* followed at some distance. As Dewey's column steamed in single file towards Manila Bay, all lights were masked, with the exception of a single stern light for the following ship to navigate by. A few hours before midnight, the US

Dewey on the open bridge of *Olympia* during battle. From left to right: Samuel Ferguson (apprentice signal boy), John A. McDougall (Marine orderly), Dewey, and Chief Yeoman Merrick W. Creagh. According to *Olympia*'s Lieutenant Ellicott, "In the early dawn, Manila Bay was like a sheet of silver." (Donation of C. J. Dutreaux, NHHC NH 52830)

ships went to general quarters and crews manned their guns. Aboard *Olympia*, Commodore Dewey and Lieutenant Calkins stood on the open bridge, while *Olympia*'s Captain Gridley took his station one deck directly below, inside *Olympia*'s armored conning tower.

The mouth of Manila Bay is nearly 10 miles wide and has two possible entrances. The northern route, Boca Chica, is merely 2 miles wide and lies between the Bataan Peninsula and the island of Corregidor. The second option, Boca Grande, lies to the south, between the small Caballo Island and the islet of El Fraile. Caballo lays immediately southeast of Corregidor, while El Fraile is 2 miles off Luzon, separated by shallow water. Boca Grande itself is 3 miles wide and was covered by 17 Spanish field pieces. It was Boca Grande that Dewey chose to enter.

However, Dewey's intelligence suggested only three 5.9in guns on Caballo and three 4.7in guns on El Fraile were modern breech-loaders, and they probably had an effective range of 1½nm. Dewey considered that at most they may give his squadron "a very unpleasant quarter hour."

At 2330hrs on April 30, Dewey's Asiatic Squadron began slipping into Manila Bay via Boca Grande. As the squadron penetrated the channel, it turned north–northeast to avoid shoals ahead. However, as *McCulloch* overtook El Fraile, a fiery plume erupted from its funnel. "Well," claimed an *Olympia* officer, "if someone don't see that, the whole island must be asleep." Corregidor, the Caballo islands, and the San Nicolas Banks were completely dark, the Spaniards having extinguished all lights.

Baltimore's Captain Dyer observed that Dewey was "an old hand at crossing mine fields and figured that if there was a gate through this it would be close to the rock [Corregidor]." As a Farragut admirer and disciple, Dewey despised mines, calmly announcing to his squadron, "If there are any mines in our path, the flagship will clear them away for you." Dewey believed the rumor of naval mines was a Spanish ruse to discourage a penetration of Manila Bay, and in any case, the warm saltwater would have long corroded them to uselessness. Nevertheless, Dewey recalled, "As we moved past Corregidor, not fifty yards to the right, there was a muffled roar, and a column of water shot upward thirty or forty feet high… In a moment another to my left. 'So the place is mined,' I said to Lamberton."

At 0010hrs on May 1, *Raleigh*'s skipper observed a signal rocket flashing from the mouth of the bay, and five minutes later, at 0015hrs, a single shot rang out from the El Fraile battery of 4.7in guns. The Spanish round passed diagonally between *Raleigh* and *Petrel*, missing the Americans entirely. *Boston*, *Concord*, *Raleigh*, and *McCulloch* all opened fire on El Fraile. Two more Spanish shells landed near *McCulloch* before El Fraile was silenced by between eight and ten American rounds. The US squadron continued deeper into the once again silent bay. Manila lay 25nm ahead, its electric lighting visible on the horizon.

Olympia's battle ensign that flew at Manila Bay on May 1, 1898. The cotton flag's 1898 canton only has 36 stars, while the reverse of the hoist is stamped "U.S.S. OLYMPIA MANILA BAY MAY 1 1898." (NHHC 1963-318-A)

The descent into Manila Bay, May 1, 1898

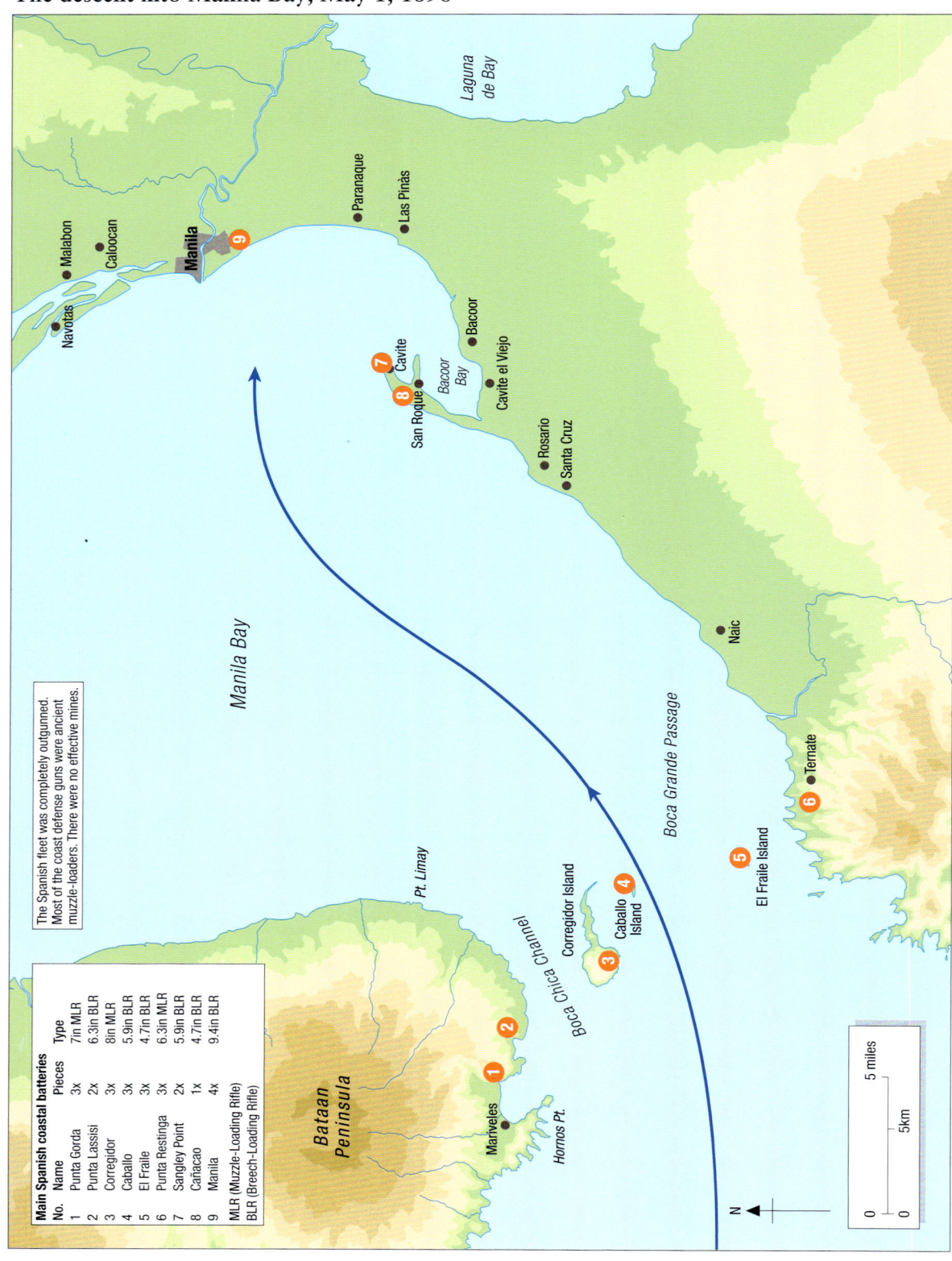

Main Spanish coastal batteries

No.	Name	Pieces	Type
1	Punta Gorda	3x	7in MLR
2	Punta Lassisi	2x	6.3in BLR
3	Corregidor	3x	8in MLR
4	Caballo	3x	5.9in BLR
5	El Fraile	3x	4.7in BLR
6	Punta Restinga	3x	6.3in MLR
7	Sangley Point	2x	5.9in BLR
8	Cañacao	1x	4.7in BLR
9	Manila	4x	9.4in BLR

MLR (Muzzle-Loading Rifle)
BLR (Breech-Loading Rifle)

The Spanish fleet was completely outgunned. Most of the coast defense guns were ancient muzzle-loaders. There were no effective mines.

Aboard *Olympia*, coffee was served to all officers and men at 0400hrs. Dawn was beginning to break. By now, the US column proceeded northeastwards, and Dewey's unarmed colliers *Nanshan* and *Zafiro* were detached to loiter safely in the middle of the bay, accompanied by the cutter *McCulloch*. As the Americans steamed deeper into Manila Bay and directly for Manila, a surprised Dewey found 16 merchantmen anchored off the city and its considerable coastal batteries, but no warships. Skirting the Manila Bay coastline, Dewey now changed course to the southwest, assuming Montojo had to be at Cavite. Aboard *Olympia*, Dewey ordered Gridley, "Take her close along the five-fathom line."

Shortly before 0500hrs, as Dewey's squadron found itself due west of Manila, American lookouts suddenly sighted Montojo's warships off Cavite. Montojo, ever mindful of casualties, had chosen not to anchor off Manila, believing it would "provoke the enemy to bombard the plaza, which doubtless would have been demolished." Montojo had instead stationed his force at the Cavite arsenal, specifically Cañacao Bay, 8 miles southwest of Manila in the lee of the Cavite peninsula. Unlike Dewey's smart column, Montojo's squadron was anchored in an irregular northeast–southwest crescent across the mouth of Bacoor Bay. The southwesternmost ships, cruisers *Don Antonio de Ulloa* and *Don Juan de Austria*, were anchored in shoal water in Cañacao Bay. In the flotilla's center were cruisers *Castilla* and *Isla de Cuba*, while flagship *Reina Cristina* and gunboat *Marques del Duero* and cruiser *Isla de Luzón* comprised the northeastern portion of Montojo's squadron. Cruiser *Velasco* and gunboat *General Lezo* were anchored alone to the south of the Cavite peninsula. Even for a squadron huddled defensively, Montojo's warships were poorly positioned, as only two 5.9in and one 4.7in gun could be brought to bear from shore batteries.

At 0500hrs, the US column turned to starboard, initially paralleling the Luzon coast in a gentle arc before bearing down on Montojo's line. Five minutes later, at 0505hrs, *Olympia* hoisted "Prepare for general action." Simultaneously, Spanish coast artillery opened on Dewey's ships, but their shots fell behind the US column without scoring any hits. One minute later, at 0506hrs, two mines exploded several miles ahead of the Americans. "Evidently the Spanish are already rattled," Dewey observed. As the Americans passed, *Concord* and *Boston* fired several retaliatory shots, but then both Spanish artillery and the two US ships again fell silent.

The Spaniards' Sangley Point battery opened fire on the US column at 0515hrs but fell short. Meanwhile, Montojo's squadron began a weak fire of their own, hurling their shells harmlessly over the Americans. This briefly inspired *Petrel* to return several shells without orders. Otherwise, the US squadron remained silent, as Dewey wished to close the range and make his limited ammunition count.

A color chromolithograph of the Manila Bay battle, published by Muller, Luchsinger & Co in 1898. The crushing and unexpectedly one-sided US victory over a fading Old World empire caught the American zeitgeist like few other individual battles before or since, and inspired vast amounts of popular culture souvenirs. (Muller, Luchsinger & Co., LOC)

At 0522hrs, Dewey leaned into the open bridge's voice pipe and finally announced, "You may fire when you are ready, Gridley." *Olympia* was still 5,500 yards distant, and only at 0534hrs did *Olympia*'s forward 8in turret open fire, followed shortly afterwards by the cruiser's rapid-firing 5in battery. "We at once bore down on them," Gridley wrote the next day, "this ship leading." Following astern of *Olympia*, *Baltimore* opened fire at 6,000 yards with the port battery. Dewey's remaining warships followed suit as battle was joined.

At about 0545hrs, Dewey's column completed its starboard turn and pulled parallel to the Spanish line, heading northeast–southwest. Over the next hour and 45 minutes, Dewey's squadron would execute five methodical, almost leisurely clockwise loops, bombarding both the Spanish ships and fortifications at Cavite with alternating starboard and port broadsides.

As day broke, throngs of unengaged Filipino, Chinese, and Spanish civilians climbed the Manila walls and other highpoints to observe the battle firsthand. Despite the unprecedented entertainment, most probably did not like the direction the battle appeared to be unfolding. The US column maintained a deliberate and methodical fire, cruising serenely in line parallel to Montojo's line. Although the American fire was not terribly accurate, it was heavy and began scoring damaging hits against Montojo's ships almost immediately. The Spanish return fire, Dewey observed, was "vigorous, but generally ineffective."

At some point early in the engagement, a Spanish launch emerged and closed directly towards *Olympia*. The small boat potentially carried torpedoes – weapons far more dangerous than any gun battery. An accompanying civilian journalist notified Dewey of the dangerously approaching craft. "You look after her," Dewey responded. "I have no time to bother with torpedo boats. Let me know when you've finished her."

The Spanish boat was accordingly repulsed by *Olympia*'s heavy secondary battery fire. It retreated out of range, then courageously charged back towards the flagship. However, *Olympia* hit the boat several times, forcing it to retire once again and run itself aground on the beach, with even *Olympia*'s shipboard marines taking rifle potshots at it. Lieutenant Calkins observed that "Had there been a half dozen real torpedo-boats in Manila Bay in the hands of fearless and skilled officers, the whole situation would have been transformed."

USS *Olympia* leads the Asiatic Squadron into battle. The USN's overwhelming victory at Manila Bay would lead directly to the American annexation of three major Pacific territories: the Philippines, Guam, and – almost virtually forgotten now – the future US state of Hawaii. (NHHC NH 85768 KN)

Once Sangley Point was abeam of *Olympia*, Dewey ordered a 180-degree turn. At 0620hrs, *Olympia* turned to starboard, with the US column following behind it. Dewey's battle line now again steamed past the Spanish line in the opposite direction, heading back northeast about 3,000 yards from the Spaniards. Meanwhile, the inaccurate Spanish counterfire was unlucky even when it did hit, sometimes causing dramatic superficial damage against American hulls and rigging but scoring no critical hits.

After completing its second firing pass, the US squadron again came about and began a third pass, again heading southwest towards Sangley Point, and slightly closing the range. The Spanish ships continued to take critical damage, while the US ships shrugged off what few hits they received.

Dewey then turned about once more, heading northeast yet again and beginning a fourth pass. The Americans' high discipline and training contrasted sharply with that of the Spaniards. According to Lieutenant Ellicott: "It was evident that Dewey's watchful eye was upon us. From time to time a vessel's call letter would be displayed with the brief signal: 'Close up.'"

Around 0700hrs, Montojo ordered his flagship *Reina Cristina* to charge the US squadron. *Reina Cristina* pulled out of the Spanish line and was immediately brought under heavy American fire, Dewey commenting that all of *Olympia*'s batteries were concentrated on it. It was a gallant but utterly hopeless, if not suicidal, gesture by a humanitarian admiral who perhaps desired one last chance to prove he personally was not a coward.

Montojo observed the three forward-most US cruisers concentrate their fire on *Reina Cristina*, which was predictably hammered by American shells. Shortly after the general action had begun, an American shell had exploded in *Reina Cristina*'s forecastle, knocking all four rapid-fire cannon crews out of action and shattering the forward mast. With the bridge helmsman wounded by mast splinters, Lieutenant José Nuñez coolly took the wheel for the remainder of the battle.

However, by 0725hrs, *Reina Cristina* was ablaze. Five minutes later, another American shell obliterated *Reina Cristina*'s steering gear. With the rudder out of action, Montojo ordered the flagship steered by hand. Yet the American bombardment against the Spanish flagship continued. Another US shell detonated on *Reina Cristina*'s poop deck and knocked nine more men out of action. Yet another strike destroyed the mizzen masthead, bringing down the Spanish flag and Montojo's personal ensign; both were replaced immediately.

More shells continued to slam into the Spanish flagship as the range closed to a mere 1,200 yards. *Olympia*'s Captain Gridley specifically reported *Reina Cristina* being "raked fore and aft" by *Olympia*, including at least one hit by an 8in shell. One of the American rounds unfortunately landed in *Reina Cristina*'s officers' mess, where the ship's wounded were being treated, killing everyone present. Another American round detonated astern in *Reina Cristina*'s ammunition room and began to fill the after part of the ship with smoke, preventing *Reina Cristina* from being steered by hand. The blaze became impossible to

Dewey's location atop *Olympia*'s open flying bridge during the battle has been memorialized on the preserved *Olympia* in Philadelphia. On September 11, 1957, the USN transferred *Olympia* to the independent Cruiser Olympia Association. *Olympia* reopened to the public on October 6, 1958. (Author's collection)

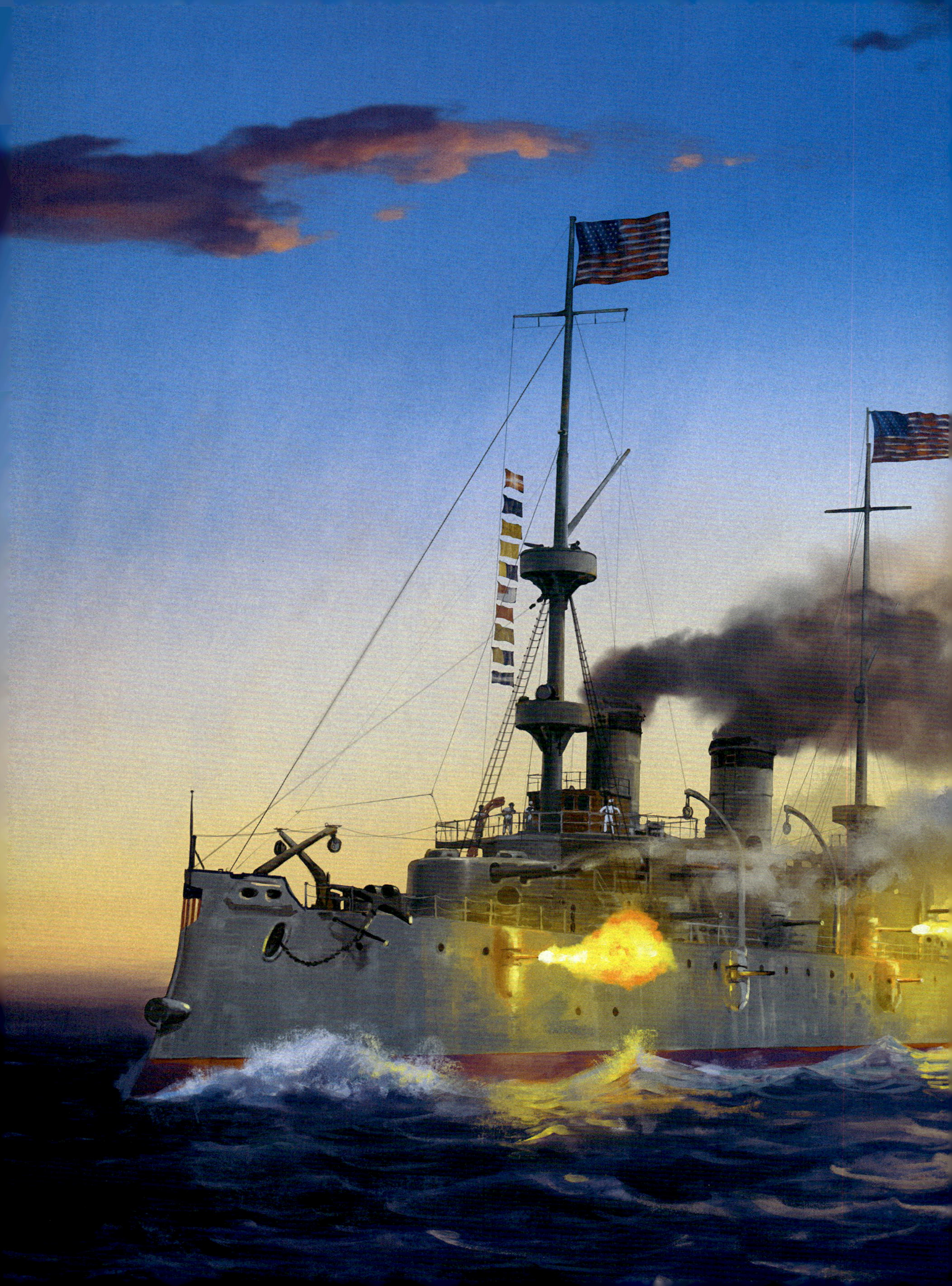

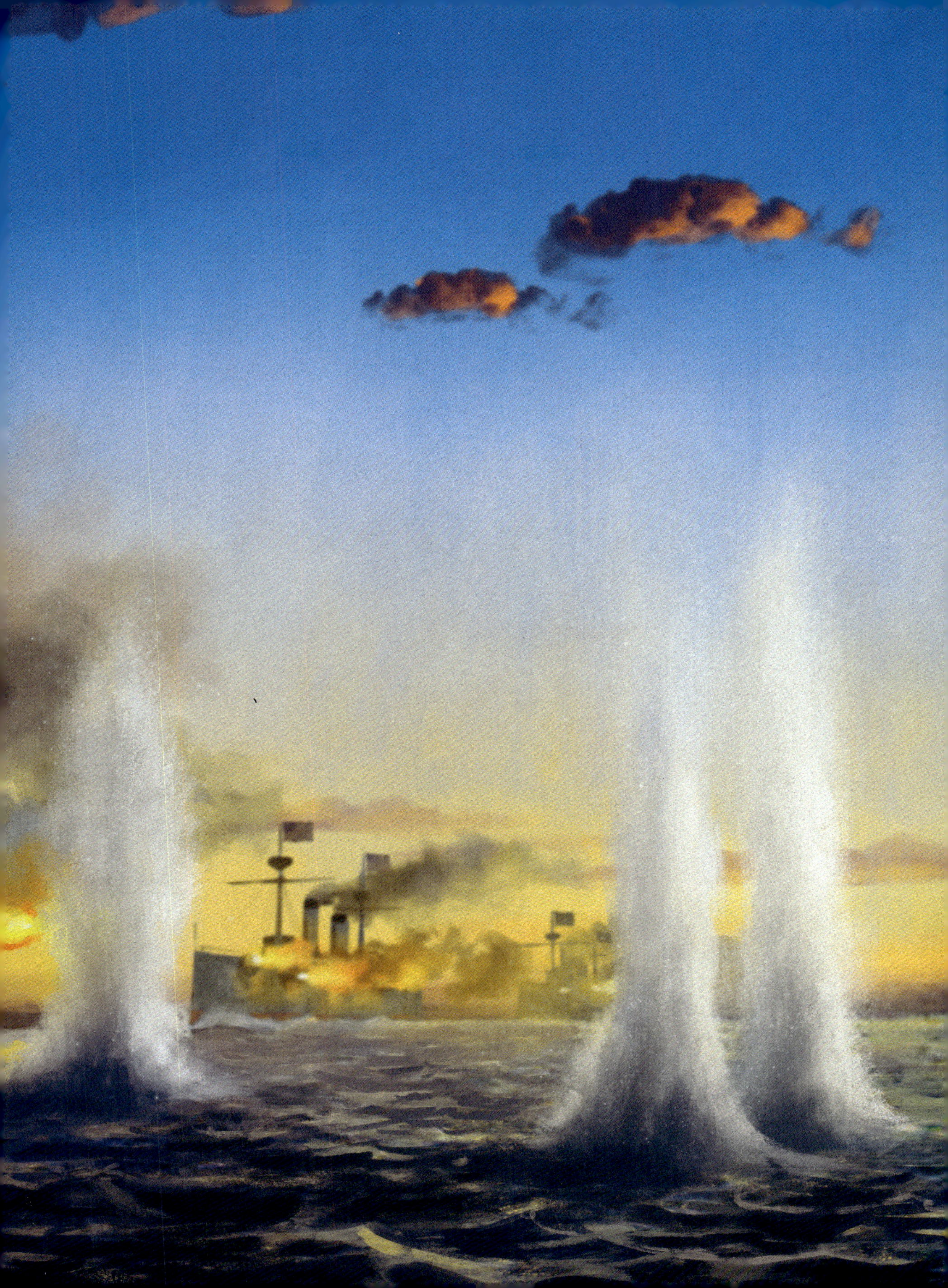

USS *OLYMPIA* LEADS THE ASIATIC SQUADRON INTO BATTLE, MAY 1, 1898 (PP.46–47)

Dewey appeared on the flying bridge wearing his white commodore's uniform and – allegedly – a golfing cap. Dewey later claimed his commodore's cap had gotten lost, but this was quite possibly a purposeful attempt to project casual confidence to his men. Despite his calm demeanor, Dewey was feeling the tension of the moment. He reportedly was unable to keep down anything he ate or drank.

Although *Olympia* included a dedicated admiral's quarters in its stern, there was no admiral's level armored conning tower. While Captain Gridley conned *Olympia* one deck below behind several inches of armor, Dewey was forced to stand on the flying bridge in the open. No doubt this arrangement was secretly preferred by glory-seeking admirals.

Immediately below Dewey's feet was Gridley in the armored conning tower. Although gravely ill and scheduled to be transferred home, Gridley had begged Dewey for the chance to stay and fight in the upcoming war. Gridley was known for his "quiet, dependable attention to duty" as well as a "certain decency and consideration in his dealings with others regardless of their position or status in life."

At 0522hrs, Dewey gave Gridley permission to open fire at his discretion. *Olympia* opened fire 12 minutes later at 0534hrs **(1)**. It was immediately followed by the rest of Dewey's squadron **(2)**. Over the next two hours, Dewey's Asiatic Squadron would make five gunnery passes against Montojo's warships and coastal batteries at Cavite, inflicting significant damage while absorbing only superficial damage in return.

control. Eventually, Spanish rounds began to detonate, forcing Montojo to flood *Reina Cristina*'s magazine.

Montojo later reported: "The ship being beyond saving, with the hull, smokestack, and mast pierced repeatedly, with the cries of the wounded echoing, with half the crew – including seven officers – down, I gave the order to scuttle her before the magazines went off." *Isla de Cuba* and *Isla de Luzón* now came alongside the stricken *Reina Cristina* to take off the wounded. Meanwhile, the remorseless Americans kept scoring hits on *Reina Cristina*.

Around 0735hrs, Montojo was forced to transfer his flag from *Reina Cristina* to *Isla de Cuba*, all while still under heavy American fire. According to a British merchantman captain: "During that perilous passage of a mile or more, Montojo stood upright in the stern perfectly unmoved, although splashes of water flew repeatedly over the little craft… It was an example of unparalleled heroism." Meanwhile, *Reina Cristina*'s gravely wounded skipper, Capitan Luis Cadarso, stayed behind to ensure every survivor could get off the ship. Cadarso ultimately died of his injuries.

Around 0730hrs, Dewey had turned about and begun his fifth pass against the Spanish, now heading northeast–southwest again. Within moments, however, Dewey suddenly received an apparently garbled report from Captain Gridley claiming that only 15 rounds per gun remained for *Olympia*'s rapid-fire 5in battery. "It was a most anxious moment for me," Dewey later recalled. Despite the damage the Americans had visibly done to the Spanish, the battle did not seem decided. Indeed, Dewey felt that the Spanish ammunition was apparently as "ample as ours was limited," and he was always aware his squadron was far from home. *Olympia*'s assistant surgeon carpenter remarked that, "It did seem as if we had wasted a lot of ammunition, for the true state of affairs was not evident until later."

At 0735hrs, a concerned Dewey ordered the entire US squadron to cease fire and pull away to relative safety deeper into Manila Bay while he considered his tactical options. "Let the people go to breakfast," Dewey cleverly explained, ordering his ship captains to board *Olympia* at 0840hrs for a conference. It was during this lull that Dewey discovered the true message: *Olympia* had only *fired* 15 shells per 5in gun.

Meanwhile, the severely worked-over Spanish had also ceased fire. As the commotion died down and the smoke cleared, the true damage to Montojo's

Modern-day view from *Olympia*'s flying bridge, looking over *Olympia*'s forward twin 8in turret towards the bow. Except for the peacetime ocher turrets and superstructure, the view is largely as Dewey and his lieutenants would have seen it. (Author's collection)

EVENTS

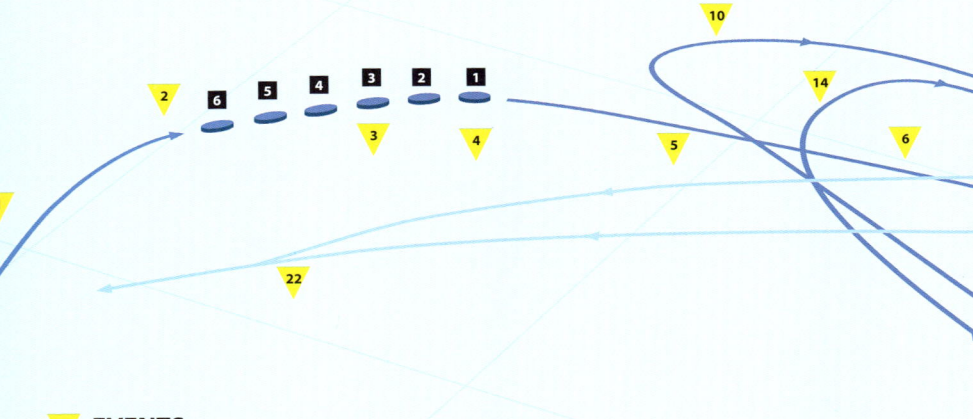

1. US Asiatic Squadron sights Montojo's squadron shortly before 0500hrs.
2. Asiatic Squadron turns to starboard at 0500hrs, bearing directly for Montojo's warships.
3. Spanish coastal artillery opens fire at Asiatic Squadron at 0505hrs.
4. Two Spanish naval mines explode several miles ahead of the Asiatic Squadron at 0506hrs.
5. Montojo's warships and Sangley Point battery open fire at Asiatic Squadron at 0515hrs. *Petrel* briefly returns fire without orders.
6. At 0522hrs, Dewey announces aboard *Olympia*, "You may fire when you are ready, Gridley."
7. *Olympia* opens fire with its 8in guns at 0534hrs. Dewey's remaining warships follow suit.
8. *Olympia* repulses apparent torpedo boat attack.
9. At 0620hrs, *Olympia* leads the US Asiatic Squadron about for a second firing pass at a range of about 3,000 yards.
10. US Asiatic Squadron turns about for its third firing pass.
11. US Asiatic Squadron turns about for its fourth firing pass.
12. At 0700hrs, Montojo orders *Reina Cristina* to charge US column.
13. By 0730hrs, the charging *Reina Cristina* has been crippled by a hail of American fire from just 1,200 yards.
14. US Asiatic Squadron begins its fifth firing pass around 0730hrs.
15. *Isla de Cuba* and *Isla de Luzón* come alongside crippled *Reina Cristina* as Montojo is forced to transfer his flag.
16. After receiving an inaccurate report that *Olympia* is low on ammunition, at 0735hrs, Dewey orders the US squadron to cease fire and retreat out of range while he confers with his officers.
17. Montojo orders his surviving ships to retreat into Bacoor Bay and prepare to scuttle if necessary. *Lezo*, *Duero*, *Manila*, *Velasco*, and *Argos* all run themselves ashore.
18. Dewey orders his squadron to return to the attack at 1116hrs, led this time by *Baltimore*, which closes to within 2,200 yards of the Cavite guns and *Don Antonio de Ulloa*, eventually coming to a full stop entirely to engage the Spanish.
19. At 1145hrs, Dewey orders *Concord* to destroy *Mindanao*. *Concord* closes within 2,500 yards and commences a heavy fire.
20. At 1200hrs, *Raleigh* attempts to get into the inner harbor to help wipe out the remaining Spanish ships. After finding itself in 20ft of water, *Raleigh* is forced to withdraw.
21. *Petrel* bombards Cavite and Spanish ships sheltering behind the mole, before observing a white flag run up at 1230hrs. *Petrel* reports this to *Olympia* and the US Asiatic Squadron ceases firing.
22. US Asiatic Squadron temporarily withdraws into Manila Bay.

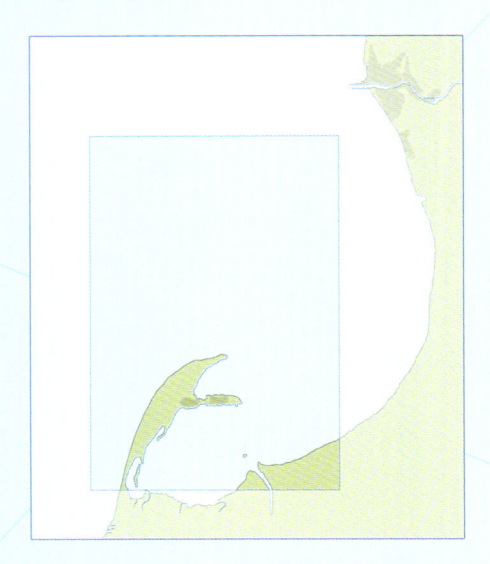

SPAIN
Escuadrón del Pacífico – Contraalmirante Patricio Montojo y Pasarón
A. Unprotected cruiser *Reina Cristina* (F)
B. Unprotected cruiser *Castilla*
C. Protected cruiser *Isla de Cuba*
D. Protected cruiser *Isla de Luzón*
E. Unprotected cruiser *Don Antonio de Ulloa*
F. Unprotected cruiser *Don Juan de Austria*
G. Gunboat *Marques del Duero*
H. Gunboat *General Lezo*
I. Unprotected cruiser *Velasco*
J. Gunboat *El Cano* (off map)
K. Gunboat *Argos*
L. Transport *Manila*
M. Transport *Mindanao*
N. Steamer *Isla de Mindanao*

BATTLE OF MANILA BAY, MAY 1, 1898
The US Asiatic Squadron destroys its Spanish counterpart.

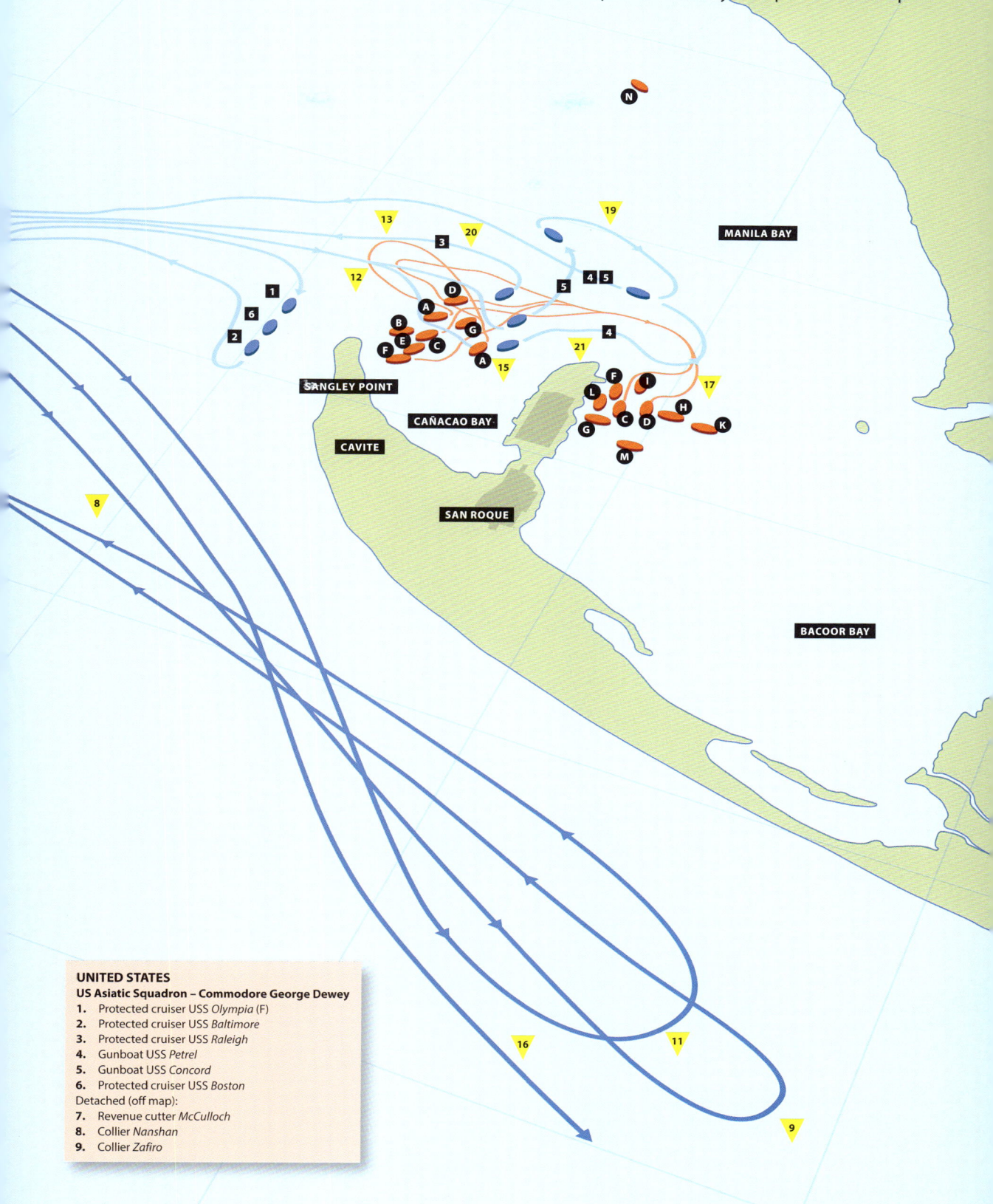

MANILA BAY

SANGLEY POINT

CAÑACAO BAY

CAVITE

SAN ROQUE

BACOOR BAY

UNITED STATES
US Asiatic Squadron – Commodore George Dewey
1. Protected cruiser USS *Olympia* (F)
2. Protected cruiser USS *Baltimore*
3. Protected cruiser USS *Raleigh*
4. Gunboat USS *Petrel*
5. Gunboat USS *Concord*
6. Protected cruiser USS *Boston*

Detached (off map):
7. Revenue cutter *McCulloch*
8. Collier *Nanshan*
9. Collier *Zafiro*

squadron became evident. "It was clear that we did not need a very large supply of ammunition to finish our morning's task," Dewey later stated. As the Americans temporarily withdrew, Montojo ordered his surviving ships to retreat into the shallows of Bacoor Bay and prepare to scuttle if necessary. The Spanish gunboats *Lezo*, *Duero*, *Manila*, *Velasco*, and *Argos* – all heavily damaged – ran themselves ashore at Cavite Viejo.

Three batteries at Manila had kept up a consistent fire against the Americans, but Dewey's vessels had not responded in kind. Eventually, Dewey signaled to the governor-general that if the batteries did not cease firing, the Americans would begin to bombard the city itself. This caused the Manila batteries to fall silent.

Having taken care of necessary business without interference from the Spanish, it was now time for Dewey's squadron to finish the job. At 1055hrs, *Olympia* signaled, "Designated vessel will lead" and then ran up *Baltimore*'s pennant. At 1116hrs, Dewey ordered his squadron to return to the attack, focusing on the Spanish shore batteries and shore fortifications. *Baltimore* now led *Boston* and *Olympia* in column into a position off the Cañacao and Sangley Point batteries before opening fire with its starboard battery at a range of 2,800 yards.

Baltimore closed to within 2,200 yards and dropped to dead slow, finally stopping the engines as its gunners obtained the range. *Baltimore* now delivered "a rapid and accurate fire" into the shore batteries and *Don Antonio de Ulloa*, "practically silencing the batteries in question," according to Dyer's later report.

Raleigh made full speed to keep up with *Olympia* but "it was found to be impossible," *Raleigh*'s captain reported. "Falling behind all the time, I cut across to gain line abreast of Cavite Battery just as the flagship passed the *Baltimore* at that port, at which time we opened fire with all guns." According to Montojo, "The enemy returned, forming a circle to destroy the arsenal and the ships which remained to me, opened upon them a horrible fire, which we answered as far as we could with the few cannon which we still had mounted."

At 1100hrs, the gunboat *Petrel* had departed its station and passed outside of *Baltimore*, eventually rounding Sangley Point some 500 yards

Battalla de Cavite by Ildefonso Sanz Doménech depicts the Spanish squadron during the action. *Don Juan de Austria*, *Isla de Cuba*, and *Isla de Luzón* were all salvaged and served in the USN until 1912, 1919, and 1919, respectively. *Marques del Duero* was salvaged, renamed *P-17*, and scrapped in 1900. However, the irreparable *Don Antonio de Ulloa* was scrapped in place. (Naval Museum of Madrid, CC BY-SA 4.0 https://creativecommons.org/licenses/by-sa/4.0, via Wikimedia Commons)

from the blazing *Castilla*. *Petrel* then directed fire at *Don Antonio de Ulloa*, before realizing its target was already sinking and abandoned.

At 1145hrs, *Concord* was ordered to destroy the Spanish transport *Mindanao*, anchored deep in shoal water. En route to the transport, *Concord* fired its batteries at Cavite and several other Spanish ships. Upon closing within 2,500 yards, *Concord* commenced a heavy fire. As soon as the first rounds struck, ten boats full of men were seen to leave *Mindanao* for the beach.

Fifteen minutes later, *Raleigh* attempted to get into the inner harbor to destroy what remained of the Spanish ships. *Raleigh* opened fire on the defiant *Don Antonio de Ulloa* and kept pouring rounds into the Spanish warship until it sank. However, *Raleigh* shortly found itself "getting into shoal water – 20 feet – and was obliged to withdraw." *Raleigh* retired and later anchored next to *Olympia*.

By now, Montojo had ordered his surviving ships scuttled, "taking care to save the flag, the distinguished pennant, the money in the safe, the portable arms, the breech plugs of the guns, and the signal codes." According to *Concord*'s skipper, by 1225hrs:

> Not a Spanish flag was flying in the harbor except from the staff of the sunken cruiser *Don Antonio de Ulloa*, submerged behind Sangley Point; the *Reina Christina* was a mass of flames and sunk near the bastion at Cavite, and the *Castilla* was burning rapidly in Cañacao Bay. The remaining vessels of the Spanish fleet sought refuge behind the arsenal and several of them were on fire; the guns at the Cavite and Sangley batteries had almost ceased firing, and a white flag appeared on the shears at the arsenal.

Meanwhile, spying masts behind the Cavite arsenal, *Petrel* put several shots through the obstructing government buildings, trying to hit the ships on the far side of the mole. Shortly afterwards, at 1230hrs, *Petrel* observed the Spanish flag over Cavite pulled down and a white flag run up in its place. *Petrel* immediately signaled that the Spanish had surrendered, and the US squadron ceased firing. Ten minutes later, at 1240hrs, Dewey's ships stood back in Manila Bay.

Battle of Manila Bay by W. G. Wood depicts *Reina Cristina* succumbing to American fire. According to an *Olympia* officer, "To breed men and waste them is the awful tradition of the Kingdom of Castile." (W. G. Wood, public domain, via Wikimedia Commons)

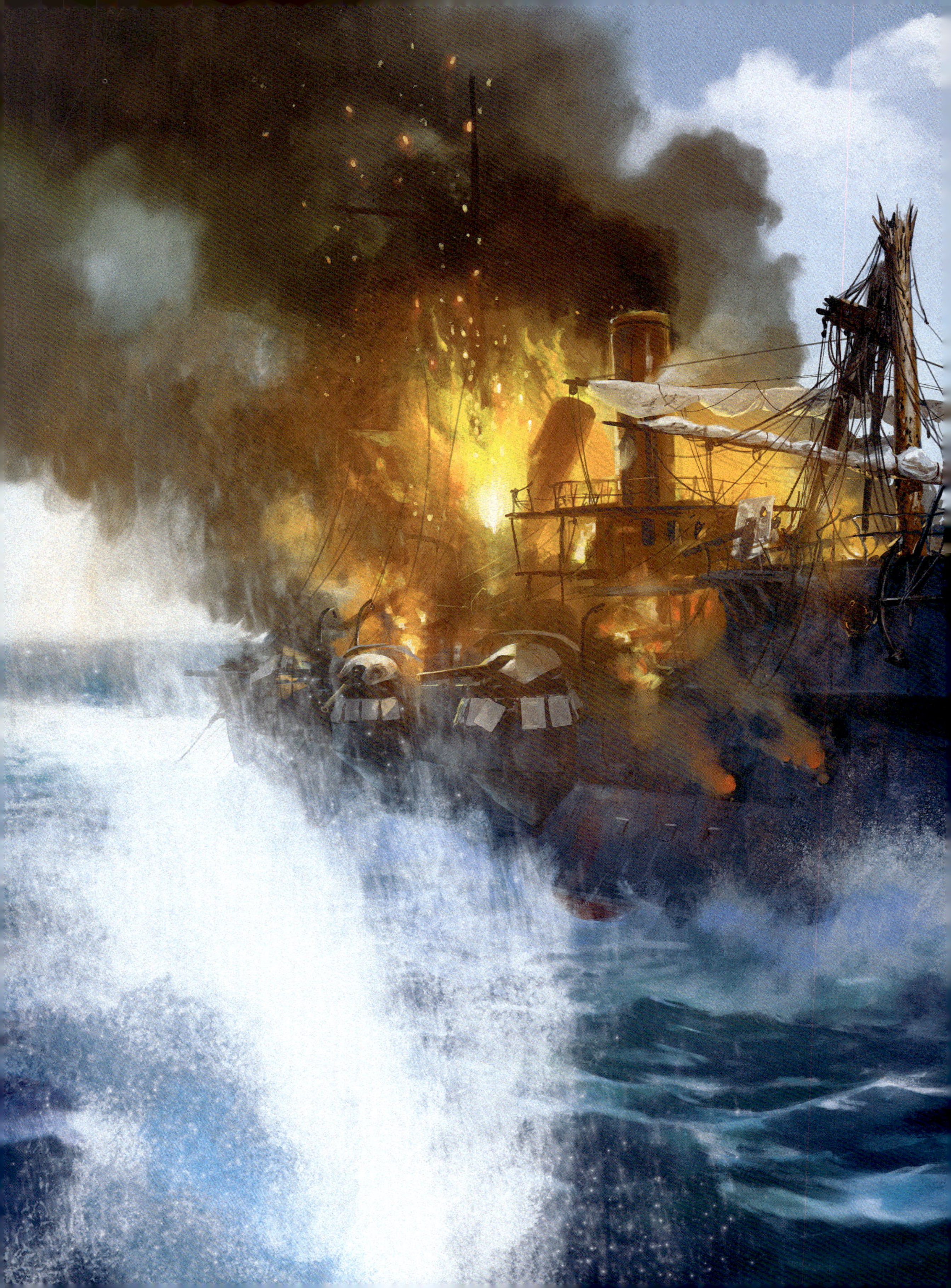

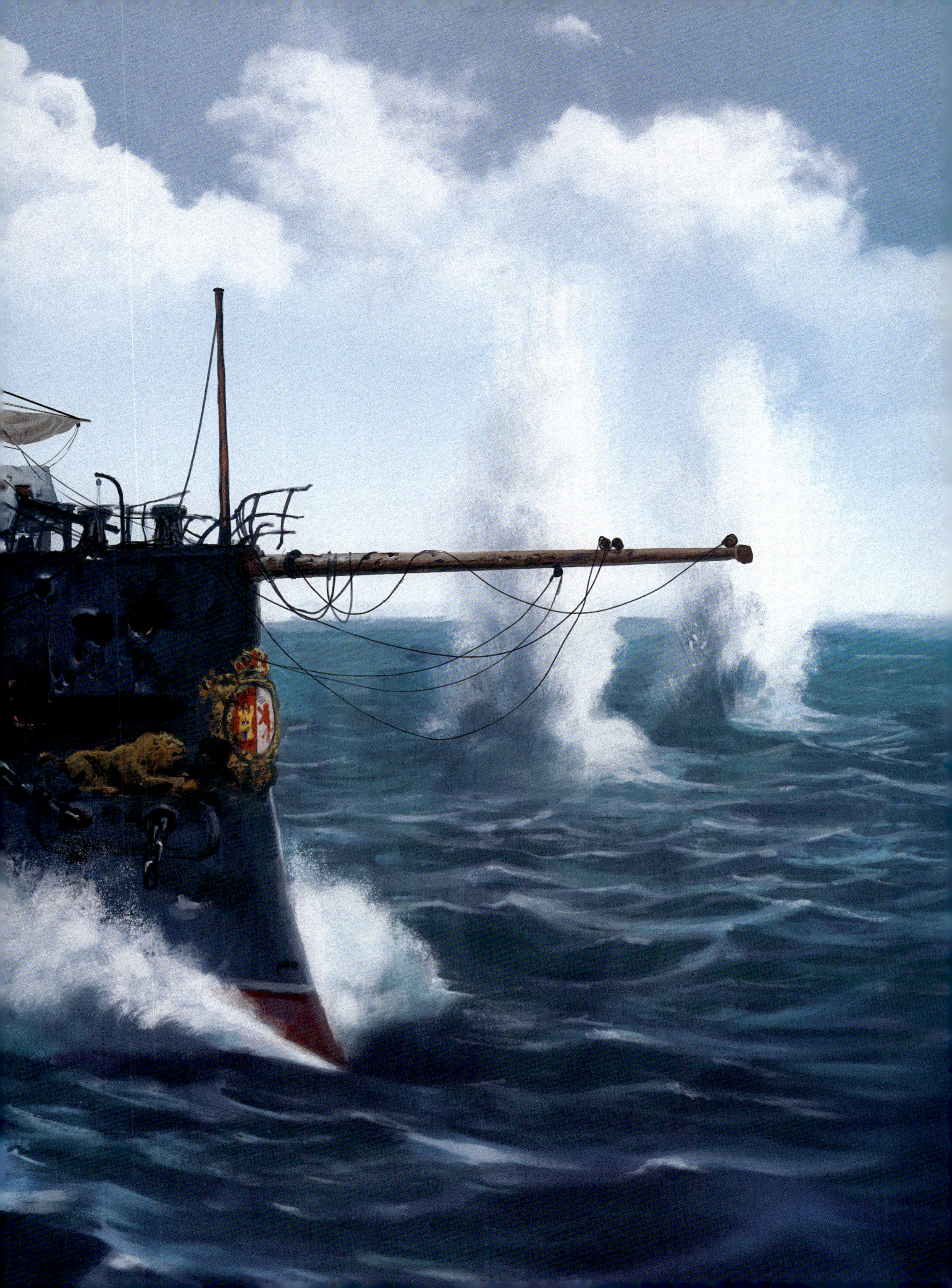

REINA CRISTINA'S LAST STAND, 0715HRS, MAY 1, 1898 (PP. 54–55)

In 1894, the small unprotected cruiser *Reina Cristina* had transferred to the Escuadrón del Pacífico to counter German attempts to annex the Caroline Islands. It shortly became the squadron's flagship **(1)** and gave naval support during the 1896–97 Filipino revolt.

At 0400hrs on May 1, *Reina Cristina*'s men were called to general quarters and given breakfast at their battle stations. Around 0445hrs, Dewey's squadron was sighted bearing down on Montojo's squadron at a distance of 3.5nm. As both squadrons opened fire on each other, *Reina Cristina* slipped its cables so that it could maneuver against the closing Americans.

At 0515hrs, all Spanish warships opened fire. The Americans returned fire at 0534hrs. Most of *Olympia*'s, *Baltimore*'s, and *Boston*'s fire was directed at *Reina Cristina*. Within moments, the Americans scored a devastating hit on *Reina Cristina*'s forecastle, which knocked out its four forward rapid-firing guns and wrecked the foremast **(2)**. Montojo later reported that "the enemy shortened the distance between us, and rectifying his aim, covered us with a rain of rapid-fire projectiles."

At 0700hrs, Montojo ordered the blazing *Reina Cristina* to charge the US column in a ramming attempt. *Reina Cristina*'s gallant but ultimately futile attempt to close the US squadron and inflict substantial damage is depicted here **(3)**.

A US shell exploded in the officers' mess, killing many wounded men being operated on. Another shell exploded in the ammunition room, disabling even the hand-steering and filling the after quarters with smoke. Half of *Reina Cristina*'s crew had been knocked out of action, and the flagship was horribly ablaze, prompting Montojo to order the ship abandoned and scuttled. *Reina Cristina*'s skipper, Captain Luis Cadarso, was mortally wounded by the second-to-last US shell to hit the ship. As the captain had been killed, the ship's after action report to Montojo was written by the wounded executive officer on May 11.

A Spanish officer at Cavite signaled for a truce that allowed the women, children, and wounded to leave. The US officer who met him observed that with the Spanish squadron destroyed his mission was complete and agreed to the truce so long as Spanish shore batteries at the mouth of the Pasig River ceased fire. Spanish officers consulted with Augustín, who agreed.

After the action had been concluded, Dewey ordered *Petrel* to burn the shattered Spanish ships that had settled in Cavite's shallow water. *Petrel* dispatched a Lieutenant Hughes and seven men in a whaleboat to finish the job. Hughes's boat crew subsequently set fire to cruisers *Don Juan de Austria*, *Isla de Luzón*, *Isla de Cuba*, and gunboats *General Lezo* and *Marques del Duero*. However, the transport *Manila* was spared, when begging Spanish officers pointed out their ship was unarmed. After carrying out this mission, *Petrel* departed Cavite and returned to Dewey's anchorage towing the small tugs *Rapido* and *Hercules*, plus three steam launches.

At 1320hrs, Dewey ordered his ships to prepare to drop anchor, and ten minutes later to "anchor at your discretion." At 1345hrs, *Concord* started to rejoin the squadron but was ordered to join *Petrel* at Cavite. As *Concord* anchored, *Petrel* signaled, "Have destroyed eight vessels here." By now, multiple white flags were flying ashore and Spanish resistance had completely ceased. The battle was effectively over.

Olympia had fired 36 8in and 281 5in shells. There were several 8in misfires due to blown fuses. Gridley reported that smoke from the 8in and 5in guns "gave considerable trouble" and that the guns' telescopic sights had to be repeatedly cleaned of powder residue during the action. In fact, US gunnery had been shockingly poor, although probably reasonable for the period. Dewey's squadron had fired 5,859 shells during the battle and scored a mere 145 hits on the seven Spanish warships engaged in the encounter – this does not include shots fired at unengaged ships or shore installations. Interestingly, the Americans' few 8in guns had performed best.

Captain Gridley's *Olympia* had absorbed perhaps five or six inconsequential hits, but no crew were significantly wounded. *Baltimore* had been the most heavily damaged US vessel, receiving a total of five hits from Spanish guns. The most serious was a 4.7in shell which struck just above the main deck and ricocheted wildly about the ship. This hit damaged various pieces of equipment and detonated several 3-pdr charges, but only eight men were claimed injured, a near miracle. *Raleigh* was struck by a single 6-pdr shell, which passed through both sides of its whaleboat and then glanced along a starboard 6-pdr gun, causing just light damage. *Boston* had suffered four hits from Spanish shells, which did "no material damage." However, the concussion of *Boston*'s own guns destroyed three of *Boston*'s boats and badly damaged three others. Amazingly, *Concord* had suffered no hits whatsoever, while *Petrel* had been hit by a single Spanish round which glanced off the hawsepipe, causing no casualties.

A photograph of a painting of gunboat USS *Petrel* under steam at Manila Bay on May 1, 1898. *Petrel* was the smallest USN warship at Manila Bay, but its heavy armament inspired its nickname "Baby Battleship." (NHHC NH 123394)

An illustration of *Petrel*'s boat crew burning crippled Spanish ships at Cavite. Only one launch was available because *Petrel*'s gun blasts had destroyed all the others. This action essentially wrote the end of the naval battle. (Drawings by C. T. Smith, *Deeds of Valor* Vol. 2, Detroit: Perrien-Keydel Co., NHHC NH 79948)

Just nine Americans were wounded, according to Dewey's official casualty report. The only reported American death was *McCulloch* Chief Engineer Frank B. Randall, who had died of a heart attack just as the squadron entered Manila Bay. However, some 150 Americans had deserted in Hong Kong before the battle, and at least one Spanish historian has suggested Dewey hid the true number of US fatalities by classifying them as deserters. Although an intriguing theory, there appears to be no supporting evidence for this.

On the Spanish side, *Reina Cristina* and *Castilla* had suffered a combined 81 hits and been sunk; *Don Antonio de Ulloa* had been hit 33 times and sunk; *Don Juan de Austria* had been hit 13 times; *Marques del Duero* was struck ten times; and *Isla de Cuba* and *Isla de Luzón* were hit five and three times, respectively. These last four ships had all been scuttled or burned. Montojo had lost a combined 161 men killed and 210 wounded.

At 1630hrs, Dewey moved his warships towards Manila itself and formally demanded the city be surrendered. Governor-General Augustín gave a predictably theatrical refusal, and Spanish authorities scuttled the transport *Cebu* in the Pasig River to block the entrance. A nonplussed Dewey was now forced to communicate with the Manila government less peremptorily. Fortunately, Manila's British consul volunteered to mediate between the two parties. Dewey then requested to use Manila's telegraph cable to communicate with his superiors. After Dewey received no reply, he declared Manila under official blockade.

By evening, Dewey's squadron was anchored directly off Manila's Luneta waterfront, where an increasingly large crowd of curious civilians had begun to gather. *Olympia*'s band suddenly struck up a concert, serenading Manila's citizens with various Spanish tunes as well as the popular "There'll Be a Hot Time in the Town Tonight," which would become an anthem of sorts for the 1898 Philippines campaign. As *Olympia*'s band played into the night, its performance was punctuated by the sudden detonation of *Don Juan de Austria*'s magazines. As one historian put it: "It was a strange end to a strange day."

THE REPUBLIC OF HAWAI'I, MARCH–MAY

The Republic of Hawai'i's pro-American oligarchy had watched the developing Spanish–American crisis with keen interest. In early 1898, as war with Spain loomed, the USN had requested additional coaling space from the Hawai'i government. Sensing renewed hope for annexation, the Republic's oligarchy had granted this on March 8.

Meanwhile, Hawai'i's American businessmen advised Republic President Sanford B. Dole that in the event of war, Hawai'i should not declare neutrality but instead put all Hawai'ian resources at the USN's disposal – a development US Secretary of State John Sherman reported to the US Senate Committee on Foreign Relations. Republic of Hawai'i minister Francis Hatch offered the Hawai'ian-flagged steamer SS *China* for USN war use, recommended the USN buy up Honolulu's entire coal stock, and urged Hawai'i's Executive Council to offer the USN a battalion of the Hawai'i National Guard for use in Cuba. Such actions would have implied undeclared Hawai'ian war with Spain.

However, in 1898, the Hawai'i National Guard numbered only 500 militiamen, meaning the Republic of Hawai'i could not even defend itself without foreign help. Fearing both Spanish naval raids and American annexation, the Hawai'ian population at large overwhelmingly preferred neutrality. Even the pro-annexationist *Pacific Commercial Advertiser*, Honolulu's leading newspaper, feared that Spanish warships in the Caroline Islands might cruise to Hawai'i and bombard Hilo and Lahaina. The American flag, it advised, should not be raised, and gunboat USS *Bennington* given 24 hours to clear port, in accordance with international law.

However, Dewey's unexpected but crushing May 1 victory at Manila Bay abruptly destroyed Spanish naval power in the Pacific. In the process, the triumph decisively removed the strongest Hawai'ian argument against openly allying with the United States.

TENSION IN MANILA BAY, MAY–JULY

Immediately after the victory, Dewey had to decide how to handle Manila, which still controlled powerful coastal artillery. Manila could be bombarded, but this was an action that would negatively affect international opinion. However, if Dewey landed in Manila to occupy it, the welfare of the city's inhabitants would immediately become his responsibility. Dewey's squadron was 7,000 miles from the nearest American port, forcing him to seize the necessary naval facilities to maintain his ships.

On May 2, Dewey demanded the evacuation of the Corregidor garrison. The Spanish complied, and the 100 men of the garrison were allowed to depart via boat for Naic. However, the Corregidor garrison commander voluntarily surrendered to the Americans, who accommodated him and his family aboard the cruiser *Baltimore*. Meanwhile, the wounded Montojo and his staff had retreated ashore. On May 2, Spanish officials in Manila informed the government in Madrid via telegraph of the Manila Bay disaster.

The wreck of *Castilla* settled in shallow water off Cavite, presumably a day or two following the naval battle. Several sunken Spanish warships were salvaged by the Americans and commissioned into USN service, but not *Castilla*. (NHHC NH 101344)

A church at Cavite shows signs of heavy damage after the naval battle. The following day, Dewey was met ashore by a group of Spanish priests and nuns, who bravely begged him for mercy on the inhabitants of Manila. (Donation of C. J. Dutreaux, NHHC USN 902950)

The streets of Madrid erupted with angry riots, requiring Spanish authorities to violently deal with demonstrators.

That same day, Dewey demanded Manila's telegraph station be turned over to the Americans, for both sides to use, or he would cut Manila's undersea cable to Hong Kong. However, the Spanish had a second, secret cable that went through the Visayas, so they allowed Dewey to drag and cut the Manila cable. Throughout the remainder of the campaign, the Manila government would still be able to communicate with Madrid almost in real-time. Dewey, however, would be forced to physically ferry all messages to Hong Kong via the cutter *McCulloch*, a frustratingly time-consuming process.

On May 4, Governor-General Augustín created an advisory council to give the Manila government a token appearance of popular representation. Among its 17 Filipino notables were several men with close ties to the Katipunan. But the council would not meet for weeks to come, and it was immediately denounced by Aguinaldo as a fraud. That same day, Augustín authorized a popular militia to fight the Americans. Up to 20,000 may have joined, but predictably, many sympathized with the insurgents and some simply defected after the Spanish trained and armed them.

Upon receiving Dewey's belated action report, McKinley observed that the problem was that the decisive battle had "taken place at Manila and not on the high seas[.] Manila became a question from which we could not escape. Dewey had to go there to find the Spanish fleet... [A]nd having destroyed their fleet Dewey found [Manila] to be the safest and indeed the only harbor excluded from all other countries['] ports." Imperialism abhors a vacuum, and it was well understood that the major European powers in Asia, particularly the Germans, were eager to occupy the Philippines once the Americans had smashed Spanish power. As a USN essay describes, in the immediate aftermath of events in Manila Bay, "the war was still in its early stages, and Dewey's situation, while secure for the moment, was still tenuous."

On May 7, Long cabled Dewey (through Hong Kong) that Dewey had been promoted to rear admiral, effective immediately. Long also asked Dewey what additional forces he required. Dewey responded: "In my best judgment, a well-equipped force of 5,000 men." According to Dewey's later testimony, he only expected to occupy Manila itself, and to do so with the assent or support of Filipinos.

On May 12, the diminutive Spanish gunboat *Callao* returned to Manila after a 15-month deployment in the southern Philippines. *Callao*'s crew was completely ignorant of what had transpired in the past few weeks. *Raleigh*, *Baltimore*, and *Olympia* all opened fire on the 208-ton *Callao*, prompting the Spanish vessel to strike its colors in surrender. The Americans took *Callao*'s crew prisoner, but soon paroled them at Cavite. However, when

Callao's paroled commander reached Manila, the Spanish government accused him of cowardice for not fighting Dewey's entire squadron. The unfortunate skipper was court-martialed and sentenced to death, but ultimately reprieved.

During the Victorian era, it was not uncommon or even impolite for neutral powers to send military missions to observe and potentially mediate foreign conflicts, so long as formal international protocol was followed. The curious British gunboat HMS *Linnet* had arrived in Manila Bay back on May 2, followed on May 5 by French armored cruiser *Bruix*. Both formally requested Dewey's permission to enter the bay, which Dewey granted, assigning each a specific anchorage, as was customary.

However, the next day, May 6, the Imperial German protected cruiser SMS *Irene* entered Manila Bay. When *Irene* refused to acknowledge American queries, a shot from *Olympia* rang over its bow. *Irene*'s captain later claimed he had been unaware Manila Bay was under blockade, although he had actually been informed by a merchantman while en route to Manila. Just hours after *Irene* arrived came the German transport *Darmstadt*, carrying 1,400 German marines of the III. Seebataillon. *Darmstadt* also ignored Dewey's instructions. Then on May 7, British cruiser HMS *Immortalité* arrived. *Immortalité*'s Captain Chichester – incidentally a close friend of Dewey's – graciously requested an anchorage, which Dewey granted.

The following day, May 8, came the small German cruiser SMS *Kormoran*. In the typical Wilhelmine fashion, it also barged its way in uninvited and earned a *Raleigh* warning shot across the bow. *Kormoran* stopped and was boarded by the Americans. Following *Kormoran* on May 10 was Japanese cruiser *Itsukushima*. Like every neutral warship not owned by the Kaiser's government, *Itsukushima* requested an anchorage, which Dewey assigned 7 miles west of Cavite.

The real German crisis began on May 12, when the Kaiserliche Marine's Vizeadmiral Ernst Otto von Diederichs, commander of Germany's Ostasiengeschwader (East Asia Squadron), arrived in Manila Bay aboard protected cruiser SMS *Kaiserin Augusta*. The sudden increase in German power in Manila Bay did not appear innocent or accidental. Von Diederichs and his staff were received warmly by Governor-General Augustín and were invited to a picnic accompanied by several Spanish generals and high military officials. After the feast, von Diederichs gave a speech declaring that so long as Wilhelm II was Kaiser, Germany would never allow the Philippines to come under American rule. Additionally, the German consul in Manila was openly sympathetic to Spain, and he frequently engaged the governor-general in consultation, while German and Spanish officers fraternized in public. Over the next several months, the German squadron under von Diederichs would maintain a relentlessly obnoxious presence in Manila Bay, refusing to acknowledge Dewey's authority or international decorum in general.

This 1898 illustration depicts the well-connected War Room in the president's Executive Mansion (the White House). The first transcontinental telegraph line across the United States had been completed in 1861, followed by the first transatlantic cable in 1866. By 1898, millions of telegrams per year were being sent across the globe through more than 3 million miles of telegraph wires and 200,000 miles of undersea cable. (NHHC)

USRC *McCulloch* fires a shot across the bow of an intruding German ship. To this day, the exact motives behind the German behavior at Manila Bay remain controversial to historians. (Frank Cresson Schell, Detroit Publishing Co., LOC)

Meanwhile, in early May, Aguinaldo – still stuck in Hong Kong – had arranged with US Consul General Edwin Wildman the securing of small arms, financed with 117,000 pesos from the Spanish pay-off deposit. Wildman eventually secured Dewey's permission for Aguinaldo to return to the Philippines, and by May 16, Aguinaldo and his men had departed Hong Kong aboard Dewey's *McCulloch*.

On May 19, *McCulloch* arrived at Manila with Aguinaldo and his officers. Aguinaldo now finally met Dewey, who somewhat patronizingly told him: "Now go ashore and start your army." The following morning, Aguinaldo began assuming command of the 30,000 Filipino rebels. In addition, Dewey gave Aguinaldo two modern field pieces, 500 rifles, and 200,000 rounds of ammunition. "I wanted his help, you know," Dewey explained later.

Meanwhile, frenetic ad hoc preparations for a US ground expedition to the Philippines had been under way – inevitable even – since news of the action in Manila Bay. Its overall commander, Major-General Merritt, had been appointed on May 12. Much argument had been made about its composition and purpose, but the expedition was officially authorized (and vaguely justified) by a McKinley telegram on May 19.

The following day, May 20, Rear Admiral Montgomery Sicard, president of the Naval War Board, advised Secretary Long how to defend Manila from the expected Spanish counterstroke. Sicard urged the shipping of artillery batteries and fortification materials to Manila Bay, along with naval mines. Sicard also suggested that coast defense monitor USS *Monterey* be dispatched to reinforce Dewey at Manila, noting that *Monterey*'s homeport of San Francisco was already adequately fortified against potential Spanish attack.

Back in the Philippines, Aguinaldo publicly announced, "I return to assume command of all the forces for the attainment of our lofty aspirations, establishing a dictatorial government which will set forth decrees under my sole responsibility." Aguinaldo added that in due time he would step down as dictator in order that democratic elections could take place. Additionally, Aguinaldo implored the Filipino rebels to cooperate with Dewey's Americans, whom he proclaimed as "redeemers" of the Philippines. "Then [Aguinaldo] began operations toward Manila," Dewey later said, "and he did wonderfully well. He whipped the Spaniards battle after battle… I knew that what he was doing – driving the Spaniards in – *was saving our troops*."

Within six days, Aguinaldo's men had captured 1,500 prisoners, including Brigadier-General Garcia Peña, forcing Dewey to implore Aguinaldo to repress reprisals against the Spanish. The Spaniards' General Monet, operating north of Manila, had seen virtually his entire force destroyed by the insurgents and had been forced to flee into Manila, which Aguinaldo and his subversives soon put under siege. However, per Dewey's directions, Aguinaldo agreed not to attack the capital directly. Nevertheless, by late May, the Filipino rebels had largely cut off supplies of food to Manila, but the capital was well stocked and throughout the months-long siege there was little threat of famine to civilians, although prices of commodities and even hotel rooms doubled.

However, conditions for Spanish troops were considerably worse. Officers largely abandoned their posts and duties, while enlisted men scrabbled for every scrap of food they could find. As the siege went on, vengeful Filipino civilians increasingly visited acts of violence on the hated and outnumbered Spaniards trapped alongside them in Manila.

Aguinaldo seemed to initially trust the Americans, particularly Dewey, believing that the United States' liberal, anti-colonial history implied the Americans had no hidden motives for the Philippines. Aguinaldo assumed that Filipino insurgents alone would assault Manila, with Dewey providing naval gunfire support. Hovering over everything was the knowledge that Dewey could unilaterally force the issue with an all-out naval bombardment of Manila. This was prevented by international sensibilities, not to mention Dewey's own morality. However, American historian Stanley Karnow observed that "The absence of guidance from Washington licensed Dewey, Merritt, and other American officials to improvise," noting that their only explicit political mission was to militarily defeat the Spanish, and that naturally meant enlisting the help of the Filipino insurgents – manipulating them with at best vague encouragements, and at worst, perhaps outright lies.

The increasingly dangerous political situation finally dawned on Washington officials. On May 26, Secretary Long warned Dewey: "It is desirable as far as possible and consistent for your success and safety not to have political alliances with the insurgents or any faction in the islands that would incur liability to maintain their cause in the future."

By late May, Aguinaldo had assembled, under his direct command, a ground force of 12,000 Filipino rebels to attack the Spanish garrison at Alapan, held by only 270 Spanish troops. In addition to these forces, Aguinaldo was supported by an additional 6,000 rebels nearby, while the Alapan garrison was indirectly supported by an additional 2,800 Spanish troops in Cavite. The grand total of all troops available came to 18,000 Filipino insurgents against just 3,070 Spanish soldiers.

The main fighting, which began on May 28, was never in doubt. The insurgents won, but lost 5,897 men killed. However, the supporting force of 2,800 Spaniards at Cavite would inevitably capitulate to the Filipinos on May 31. As June dawned, the Filipino revolutionaries controlled almost the entire Luzon countryside, with Spanish military and political power blockaded in the major cities.

On June 12, at his house at Cavite El Viejo, Aguinaldo formally proclaimed the independence of the Philippines, while Ambrosio Rianzares Bautista y Altamira read aloud in Spanish the Philippines Declaration of Independence that Bautista himself had written. Some 98 witnesses signed the document, including Colonel L. M. Johnson, a US Army officer who was present but held no official role on behalf of the United States government. Indeed, neither the United States nor Spain officially acknowledged the Declaration. Then on June 18, Aguinaldo announced the establishment of the Dictatorial Government of the Philippines, with himself formally named Dictator. Just five days later, on June 23, Aguinaldo issued a new decree dissolving the Dictatorial Government of the Philippines and establishing the Revolutionary Government of the Philippines in its place.

Vizeadmiral Ernst Otto von Diederichs, commander of Imperial Germany's East Asia Squadron. By August 13, Manila Bay was swollen not only with Dewey's reinforced squadron, but five German warships of von Diederichs' East Asia Squadron, four British warships, two French warships, and one Japanese warship. Dewey requested the foreign warships redeploy farther out so that Dewey could himself deploy to bombard Manila. All but von Diederichs' German squadron complied. (NHHC)

The Philippine Revolution in Manila Bay

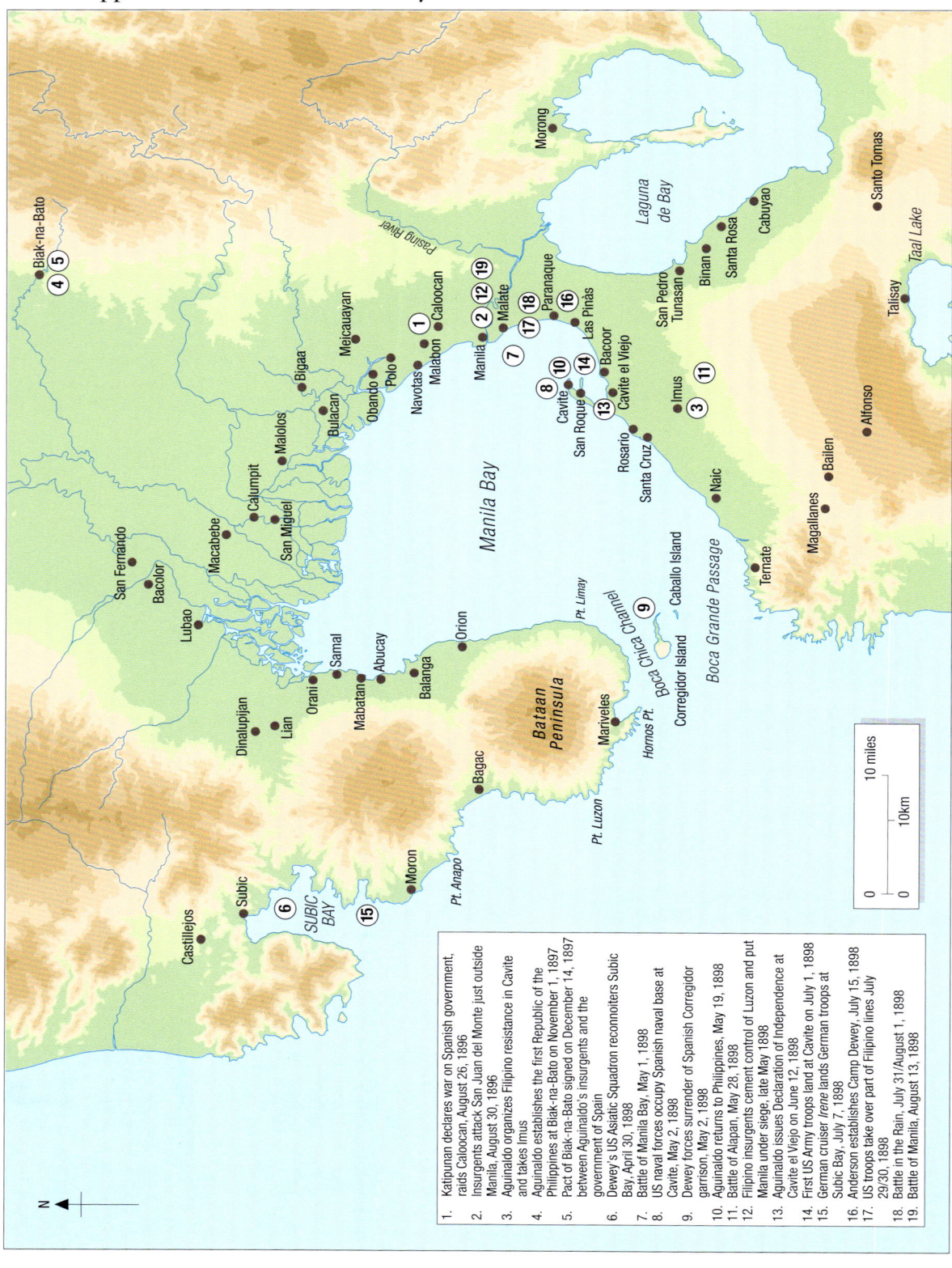

1. Katipunan declares war on Spanish government, raids Caloocan, August 26, 1896
2. Insurgents attack San Juan del Monte just outside Manila, August 30, 1896
3. Aguinaldo organizes Filipino resistance in Cavite and takes Imus
4. Aguinaldo establishes the first Republic of the Philippines at Biak-na-Bato on November 1, 1897
5. Pact of Biak-na-Bato signed on December 14, 1897 between Aguinaldo's insurgents and the government of Spain
6. Dewey's US Asiatic Squadron reconnoiters Subic Bay, April 30, 1898
7. Battle of Manila Bay, May 1, 1898
8. US naval forces occupy Spanish naval base at Cavite, May 2, 1898
9. Dewey forces surrender of Spanish Corregidor garrison, May 2, 1898
10. Aguinaldo returns to Philippines, May 19, 1898
11. Battle of Alapan, May 28, 1898
12. Filipino insurgents cement control of Luzon and put Manila under siege, late May 1898
13. Aguinaldo issues Declaration of Independence at Cavite el Viejo on June 12, 1898
14. First US Army troops land at Cavite on July 1, 1898
15. German cruiser *Irene* lands German troops at Subic Bay, July 7, 1898
16. Anderson establishes Camp Dewey, July 15, 1898
17. US troops take over part of Filipino lines July 29/30, 1898
18. Battle in the Rain, July 31/August 1, 1898
19. Battle of Manila, August 13, 1898

THE US ARMY'S PHILIPPINE EXPEDITION IS DISPATCHED TO MANILA

By early 1898, the US Army Quartermaster Department had begun preparing to transport the burgeoning US Army ground forces overseas to fight the Spanish. However, Cuba was seen as the main theater, and an expedition to the Philippines was not then seriously considered. However, Dewey's massive victory at Manila Bay had changed the American political calculus. Clearly, US troops would be needed to decisively follow up the naval victory.

According to contemporary historian Karl Irving Faust:

> Few of our people knew that there was in the United States service an officer named George Dewey, and many, and possibly the majority, had no idea where Manila was situated, or that there had been a Spanish fleet there. The first that was known of any of these things was that a Commodore Dewey had destroyed the fleet, was holding the bay, and had called for soldiers to occupy the city. Certainly he should have them. Whoever Commodore Dewey might be and wherever Manila might be could be determined later, but if there were an American like that afloat and calling for soldiers who should have what he wanted, and have it quick.

However, since the outbreak of war, the US West Coast had been virtually emptied of US Army units to transport to Cuba. Colonel Thomas M. Anderson's US 14th Infantry Regiment was the last remaining Regular unit on the West Coast. Anderson was ordered to San Francisco, promoted to brigadier-general, and put in charge of the preliminary arrangements for a Pacific-bound army, comprised mostly of militia units from the western states. Initial estimates were for 5,000 men, mainly volunteers. On May 21, Brigadier-General Anderson was put in command of the First Philippine Expedition.

Nine days later, on May 30, Major-General Wesley Merritt finally accepted command of the entire Philippine Expedition, now planned to be 20,000-strong and comprised partly of regulars. This far exceeded the "5,000 well-equipped" troops requested by Dewey to control Manila and suggests the decision to annex the Philippines had already been made by the US government. The San Francisco marshalling area was named Camp Merritt and put under the administrative control of Major-General Elwell S. Otis on June 2.

However, obtaining US merchantmen for the Pacific was necessarily more complicated than for the Atlantic and Gulf of Mexico. Most potential ships were already at sea deep in the Pacific, forcing the army to wait until they came back to port to be inspected and chartered. Additionally, the 7,000-mile voyage from the US West Coast to the Philippines would require larger transports for reasons of habitability. Nevertheless, between

The battle of Alapan marker and flag at Cavite. The battle, which took place on May 28, 1898, was the insurgents' first victory after Aguinaldo's return to the Philippines. The triumph at Alapan secured insurgent control over most of Cavite. (Mark Kevin, CC BY-SA 3.0 https://creativecommons.org/licenses/by-sa/3.0, via Wikimedia Commons)

Chartered US Army transports *City of Sydney*, *City of Peking*, and *Australia* passing out of California's Golden Gate en route first to Honolulu and then Manila Bay. In early June 1898, the editor of the highly popular news publication *Review of Reviews* noted that "A few weeks ago a great majority of the people of the United States knew nothing about the Philippines except in the vaguest possible way." (Weidner, public domain, via Wikimedia Commons)

April 25 and June 30, the US Army would charter 14 ships on the US West Coast totaling 41,152 tons displacement and a transport capacity of 629 officers and 13,059 enlisted men.

Brigadier-General Anderson's First Philippine Expedition convoy departed San Francisco for Manila on May 25, consisting of the cruiser USS *Charleston* and the transports *City of Peking*, *City of Sydney*, and *Australia*. According to Anderson: "I was ordered to Manila, when things were very unsettled, with a few regiments. I was hurried away with no explicit instructions. 'Do the best you can' were the orders I received."

This first convoy arrived at Honolulu on June 1 to a tumultuous welcome; indeed, the Hawai'ians were fond of Americans in general, and only despised the American aristocrats who had overthrown the royal government.

CAPTURE OF GUAM, JUNE 20–21

Anderson's First Philippines Expedition convoy departed Honolulu on June 4. Once at sea, Captain Henry Glass of the cruiser *Charleston* opened sealed orders from Secretary Long, dated May 10:

> You will proceed with the *Charleston* and *City of Peking* in company to Manila, Philippine Islands… On your way, you are hereby directed to stop at the Spanish Island of Guam. You will use such force as may be necessary to capture the port of Guam, making prisoners of the Governor and other officials, and any armed force that may be there… From the Island of Guam proceed to Manila and report to Rear Admiral George Dewey, U.S.N., for duty in the squadron under his command.

Captain Glass signaled Major-General Anderson aboard *Australia* his new orders to capture Guam while en route to Manila, adding that a delay of only two or three days was expected and that the transports would accompany *Charleston*.

Guam is a 210-square mile island in the Marianas archipelago. The Spanish had originally called the islands the Ladrones, before renaming them the Marianas in 1668 to honor Maria Ana of Austria, widow of Spain's King Philip IV. That same year, 1668, the Spanish established control of Guam with a Jesuit mission. About 27,000 Chamorro people lived in the Marianas in 1898, including 12,000 on Guam.

The capture of Guam

Cruiser USS *Charleston* at Agana harbor, Guam, on June 20 or 21, 1898. It is in the process of taking the surrender of the local Spanish garrison. Of the territories the United States pried from Spain in 1898, Guam certainly proved the easiest. (Collection of Rear Admiral Ammen Farenholt, NHHC NH 353)

The Americans knew there were three forts on Guam, including the ruins of ancient San Luis. In fact, a second fort, St Iago, was also old and unoccupied, leaving just a single fort, Santa Cruz, to potentially resist the Americans. Guam's total garrison consisted of 108 men – 54 Spanish regulars and 54 Chamorro volunteers. Although Glass suspected Guam was militarily weak, he prudently assumed otherwise.

The US convoy reached Guam the morning of June 20. Glass left the transports behind, out of range of Spanish guns, and charged *Charleston* into Guam's Apra harbor. After passing St Iago harmlessly, *Charleston* opened fire on Santa Cruz. After four-and-a-half minutes, a Spanish launch was observed approaching the Americans. *Charleston* checked fire, having fired a grand total of seven 3lb shells at Santa Cruz, which incidentally was also unoccupied.

When the Spanish launch reached *Charleston*, it turned out to be carrying the port's medical officer – who wished to render his services to the newcomers – and the port's embarrassed captain, who wished to apologize. Guam, he explained, had not received a ship in two years and had no ammunition with which to return the supposed gun salute. The Americans were forced to explain that their two countries were actually at war, and that they must now demand Guam's surrender.

Governor Juan Marina Vega was nonplussed that he was required to go aboard the American warship, as such action was against Spanish law. Vega replied: "I regret to have to decline this honor and to ask that you will kindly come on shore, where I await you to accede to your wishes as far as possible, and to agree to our mutual situations."

Early the following morning, June 21, *Charleston* sent a launch under flag officer Lieutenant Braunersrauther to deliver Captain Glass's terms for surrender, to which the Spanish had 30 minutes to reply. Braunersrauther's launch shortly returned with Governor Vega and the governor's handwritten note agreeing to Glass's surrender terms. The Americans took control at 1500hrs that day, ran the Stars and Stripes up Fort Santa Cruz, and issued a 21-gun salute.

Unwilling to dissipate Anderson's troops, Glass temporarily entrusted US control of Guam to Francisco Portusach, a naturalized American businessman on Guam, and José Sixto, Guam's existing Spanish treasurer. *Charleston* and the rest of the First Philippine Expedition convoy shortly departed Guam and resumed its original voyage to Manila.

CONTRAALMIRANTE CÁMARA'S SEGUNDO ESCUADRÓN, MAY–JULY

By late May, the Spanish naval minister, Ramón Aunón y Villalón, began scheming to send Cámara's Segundo Escuadrón on an offensive raid against the US East Coast. The plan was to bombard a single US port, preferably Charleston, South Carolina, and then high tail it to either San Juan in Puerto Rico or Havana or Santiago in Cuba.

Under Cámara, the Segundo Escuadrón initially comprised the armored cruiser *Emperador Carlos V*, three auxiliary cruisers, and a dispatch vessel. However, Spain's only battleship, *Pelayo*, had been under major refit at La Seyne in France since 1897. With the outbreak of war, its reconstruction was urgently accelerated. On May 14, *Pelayo* was recommissioned into Spain's Reserve Squadron to patrol the Spanish coast against potential raids, before finally being reassigned to Cámara's Segundo Escuadrón. The Armada's 4,826-ton protected cruiser *Alfonso XIII* had only been partially completed by 1896, when it was nevertheless activated for training duties. *Alfonso XIII* was assigned to Cámara's squadron and sent to Cádiz on May 7. However, upon personally observing *Alfonso XIII*'s incomplete state, Cámara refused to include it in his force. *Alfonso XIII* would remain behind in Spanish waters as a last-ditch defense for the homeland.

Back in early May, the Spanish government had dispatched Contraalmirante Pascual Cervera's decrepit cruiser squadron to Santiago, Cuba, to essentially sacrifice itself upon the altar of Spanish honor. However, by June 1, the US squadrons of Commodore Winfield Scott Schley and Rear Admiral William T. Sampson had arrived off Santiago with a combined four battleships, two armored cruisers, and numerous escorts and auxiliaries. Sampson, the senior admiral, set up a tight, aggressive blockade of Santiago, effectively bottling up Cervera's squadron in harbor. Additionally, by now, much of the remaining Cuban coast and Puerto Rico were being swarmed with flotillas of USN protected cruisers, monitors, gunboats, and auxiliaries. Finally, on June 14, a 37-ship US convoy, escorted by a fifth US battleship, departed Tampa Bay, Florida. Aboard the convoy was the US Fifth Corps, clearly bound for Cuba. The combined developments convinced Aunón that reinforcing the Caribbean was futile. The very next day, June 15, Aunón ordered Cámara's Segundo Escuadrón to the Philippines via the Suez Canal and Indian Ocean.

Cámara's Segundo Escuadrón sortied from Cádiz on June 16. Under Cámara were the battleship *Pelayo*, armored cruiser *Emperador Carlos V*, auxiliary cruisers *Patriota* and *Rapido*, torpedo boat destroyers *Audaz*, *Osado*, and *Proserpina*, transports *Buenos Aires* and *Panay* carrying a total of 4,000 troops, and four colliers loaded with a combined 20,000 tons of coal.

Cámara's squadron rounded Gibraltar on June 17 and headed for the Suez Canal. That same day, the USN learned of Cámara's sortie from Cádiz. Secretary Long notified the US State Department of Cámara's sally and directed that "the Department of State will instruct its agents, throughout the route to the East, via Suez, to throw every possible impediment in the way of coal and other necessaries being supplied to the squadron." Recognizing

During his long Armada career, Contraalmirante Manuel de la Cámara had seen action in Mexico, Peru, and Cuba prior to his service in the Spanish–American War. Cámara had been a key player in defusing the 1873 *Virginius* Affair between Spain and the United States. (NHHC)

Spanish armored cruiser *Emperador Carlos V* at Egypt's Port Said in July 1898. *Emperador Carlos V* was hurriedly commissioned on June 2, 1898 in response to the Philippines crisis. Its speed was a theoretical 20kts and the 12,000nm range at 10kts was superb. (NHHC NH 46869)

that Cámara probably expected to take on coal at Port Said, the entrance to the Suez Canal, US Consul Ethelbert Watt, on his own initiative, began buying up the port's available coal, including coal the Spanish government had already contracted for but not paid. The US government then began buying up all remaining coal east of Suez along Cámara's entire route to the Philippines.

It was in the mutual best interest of both the United States and Great Britain that Cámara's powerful force did not reach the Philippines in time to stop the Americans, and the British government, quite independently, also began throwing obstacles in Cámara's path. Although Egypt technically owned the Suez Canal, Egypt itself was under British domination. The British overlords pressured the Egyptians to recognize the strictest possible definition of neutrality, announcing that no Spanish vessel could remain at Port Said for more than 24 hours, as well as forcing Cámara to send exactly one warship at a time completely through the entire canal before the next one could be sent. This consumed 15–20 hours per ship, further slowing Cámara's progress. The final British act of frustration was to deny Cámara even the liberty of coaling his warships from his own colliers. These maneuverings slowed Cámara but did not stop him. Except for destroyers *Audaz*, *Osado*, and *Proserpina*, left behind for logistical reasons, Cámara's entire squadron passed through the Suez Canal and into the Red Sea on July 5.

Two well-escorted Spanish capital ships were now bearing down on Dewey's small and homeless squadron. Both *Pelayo* and *Emperador Carlos V* were far more heavily armed and armored than Dewey's largest and most powerful ship, *Olympia* – which was itself far more powerful than any of its consorts. Dewey clearly needed capital ships of his own, but all five US battleships were in the Caribbean. With the Panama Canal still six years away from breaking ground, no US battleship had a chance of reaching the Philippines before Cámara.

However, on June 11, the 4,084-ton monitor *Monterey* had sortied from San Francisco on a marathon voyage across the Pacific to reinforce Dewey in the Philippines. The extremely short-ranged *Monterey* was accompanied by the collier *Brutus*, which towed *Monterey* most of the way. Writing to his friend Theodore Roosevelt, US Senator Henry Cabot Lodge observed: "We are not going to lug that monitor across the Pacific for the fun of lugging her back again." Meanwhile, on June 25, monitor USS *Monadnock* had also departed San Francisco for Manila, accompanied by the collier *Nero*. Four days later, on June 29, *Monterey* and *Brutus* arrived in Honolulu.

The sortie of Cámara's squadron for the Philippines meant the Spanish homeland was largely unprotected. Therefore, on June 27, Secretary Long had ordered the formation of the Eastern Squadron, under the command of

Cámara's squadron at the Suez Canal in July 1898. The battleship *Pelayo* is in the foreground. Commissioned in 1890, *Pelayo* was under refit in early 1898 and Spanish authorities had to suspend its refurbishment in response to the war. This left *Pelayo* with its primary battery intact, but no protection for its secondary battery. (Estate of Lieutenant C. J. Dutreaux, NHHC WHI.2014.36x)

Commodore John Watson, then commanding the First Blockading Squadron off northern Cuba. The Eastern Squadron would comprise the battleships *Iowa* and *Oregon* and the auxiliary cruisers *Yankee*, *Yosemite*, and *Dixie*, all currently operating in the Caribbean. The Eastern Squadron would cross the Atlantic to directly threaten Spain itself, in the hope of diverting Cámara's squadron back to Spain. Meanwhile, the formation and purpose of the Eastern Squadron was deliberately leaked to the Spanish government by Lieutenant William Sims, a US naval attaché officer in Paris.

Meanwhile, on July 3, the combined Schley–Sampson force off Cuba thoroughly annihilated Cervera's squadron when it attempted a desperate breakout from Santiago. With Cervera's force eliminated, Secretary Long ordered the Eastern Squadron formed. Indeed, the USN had all five of its battleships off Cuba – the obsolescent but still useful *Texas* and the modern and heavily armed and armored *Indiana*, *Massachusetts*, *Oregon*, and *Iowa*. Also off Cuba were two fast and modern armored cruisers, *Brooklyn* and *New York*, and the four monitors *Puritan*, *Amphitrite*, *Miantonomoh*, and *Terror*. All 11 of these warships were a match for *Pelayo* and *Emperador Carlos V*.

However, the combined Santiago–San Juan Hill defeat clearly doomed Cuba to the Americans, meaning Madrid also anticipated the victorious US fleet soon threatening the Spanish homeland. Therefore, on July 7, just two days after so laboriously transiting the Suez Canal, the Spanish government ordered Cámara's squadron to return to Spain.

Meanwhile, Watson arrived at Guantanamo in Cuba on July 10, raised his flag on the battleship *Oregon*, and appointed *Oregon*'s Captain Charles E. Clark his chief-of-staff. Long then informed Watson that Cámara had already turned back, but the Navy Department now believed threatening Spain itself might force an end to the whole war. On July 11, Long ordered the entire North Atlantic force (except the monitors) across the Atlantic in two squadrons. Watson would command the Eastern Squadron and steam through the Mediterranean to reinforce Dewey in the Philippines. The second force, the Covering Squadron, would be commanded by Sampson and blockade the Spanish homeland to cover Watson's voyage to the Philippines.

Monitor USS *Monterey* makes its way across the Pacific during the summer of 1898. The monitors were essentially floating armored batteries capable of standing up to battleships but lacking in maneuverability. (USN photo courtesy of Darryl L. Baker via Navsource)

WAR ANNEXATION OF HAWAI'I, JULY–AUGUST

The outbreak of a major Pacific war, combined with a surge of American nationalism, made the US annexation of Hawai'i now almost certain. Hawai'i was no longer merely a potential economic boon to the United States – not controlling it had become a strategic liability.

Unlike previous annexation treaties that required a two-thirds vote in the US Senate, the proposed Newlands Resolution needed only a simple majority in each house of Congress. On July 4, the vote passed handily in both houses, and three days later President McKinley signed the Newlands Resolution into law. On July 27, Rear Admiral J. N. Miller, commander of the USN Pacific station, would steam from San Francisco in cruiser USS *Philadelphia* to take part in the official annexation ceremony. *Philadelphia* would arrive at Honolulu on August 3, joining USS *Mohican*, which was already present. Officers and men from *Philadelphia* and *Mohican* would represent the USN at the official handover ceremony at the Iolani Palace on August 12. The 1st New York arrived in Honolulu the following day, August 13, to begin establishing a US garrison.

Hawai'i had been a major part of the United States' 1898 Pacific war effort ever since the victory at Manila Bay. The formal annexation of Hawai'i mid-war ensured this would remain the case.

LAND CAMPAIGN OUTSIDE MANILA, JULY–AUGUST

Brigadier-General Thomas M. Anderson's First Philippine Expedition convoy, comprising the cruiser *Charleston* and transports *City of Peking*, *City of Sydney*, and *Australia*, arrived off Manila on June 30 and landed at Cavite the following day. Anderson's force comprised 2,500 men of the 1st California, 2nd Oregon, and elements of the 14th Infantry regiments.

Cavite and its fortifications lay on a mile-long neck so narrow that its single wagonway flooded every high tide. The Cavite neck attached to a larger, 5-mile-long peninsula, which was itself joined to the mainland. The terrain surrounding Cavite and Manila largely consisted of rough, uneven ground cut by streams and countless swamps, and covered by thick tropical vegetation. A single, often-impassable wagon road stretched 20 miles from Cavite to Manila. Farther inland, beyond the narrow, crescent-moon coastal plain, were foothills and jungled mountains reaching 7,000ft.

There was no possibility of Spanish opposition of the American landings, as the coast was totally controlled by the insurgency. By June 30, Aguinaldo's rebels were in control of Coloocan (the first station past Manila on the Manila–Dagúpan Railway) as well as the Manila suburbs of Tondo and Santa Cruz. The Filipinos had also taken control of the Santólan waterworks near San Juan del Monte, but did not cut the water supply to Manila. Indeed, as July opened, the insurgents had complete control of Luzon, apart from the Spanish government and 13,000 Spanish troops bottled up in Manila. At some point, the Filipino rebels even purchased four vessels in Singapore and armed them, but Dewey forbade them from flying their flag until the entire Philippines political issue was settled.

By the time US troops arrived, the Filipino insurgents had thrown up their own well-constructed trenches fronting Spanish lines and surrounding Manila. However, the insurgents lacked Western military discipline and often left their trenches inadequately occupied or vacated entirely. Such observations led US officers to believe that the insurgents would be utterly unreliable as an auxiliary or supporting force.

However, for the Filipino insurgents, the unexpected appearance of US ground troops was an ominous development. The day Anderson arrived, July 1, Dewey explained to Anderson: "If the United States intends to hold the Philippines Islands, it will make things awkward, because just a week ago Aguinaldo proclaimed the independence of the Philippines Islands from Spain and seems intent on establishing his own government." Over the next several days, an increasingly sullen Aguinaldo repeatedly demanded clarification of US intentions, which the evasive Dewey and Anderson were unable to give him.

Anderson chose to make his base near Paranaque. His plan was to first drive the Spanish out of their entrenchments and strongholds south and east of the walled city of Intramuros, and then to storm and capture the city itself.

Within days, the increasingly complex and unpredictable situation had become even more surreal. Back on June 20, von Diederichs' squadron in Manila Bay had been further reinforced by the protected cruiser *Prinzess Wilhelm* and the old armored cruiser *Kaiser*. Now even Aguinaldo would suffer the Germans' boorishness. Von Diederichs' increasingly brazen warships had begun landing German troops on Philippine soil on several occasions. A party of naval infantry had landed at the southern tip of Bataan, occupied the Mariveles customs house, and conducted military drills. Then on July 7, the German cruiser *Irene* landed naval infantry at Isla Grande, a Spanish naval station in Subic Bay currently under siege by the insurgents. Aguinaldo, nervous at facing the Germans alone, requested help from Dewey, who dispatched *Raleigh* and a troop-laden transport to Subic Bay. Upon seeing the American show of force, *Irene* and its men departed. The Spanish had actually been trying to surrender to the Germans, and they now surrendered to the Americans, who immediately turned them over to the insurgents. An increasingly incensed Dewey made a formal protest to von Diederichs.

Brigadier-General Thomas M. Anderson had fought in the American Civil War, on the frontier in the Red Cloud War, and was serving in Skagway, Alaska, during the Klondike Gold Rush in 1898 when the Spanish–American War broke out. Anderson's First Philippine Expeditionary Force would be the first US troops to sortie from the United States and the first to land in the Philippines following the May 1 naval victory. Anderson then requested assignment to a combat theater. (Public domain, via Wikimedia Commons)

On July 10, von Diederichs responded by sending one of his officers, Commander Paul von Hintze, to the *Olympia* to protest that *Irene* had been acting legally and that the Americans had no right to interfere. At this point, the normally imperturbable Dewey blew up, shouting, "Does Admiral von Diederichs think he commands here or I? Tell your admiral that if he wants war, I am ready." Thoroughly chastised, von Diederichs' German East Asia squadron remained in Manila Bay, but never again did it so brazenly challenge Dewey's authority.

According to Faust:

> After grave investigation, [this] writer thinks that the Germans... at no time had serious thoughts of opposing the American control of the Philippine Islands, or of causing any friction between the United States and Germany. The German commander was undoubtedly using what in other countries is called diplomacy, but in our country is called, "bluff". If the bluff had worked the officer would have been promoted; it failed and he was recalled.

On July 15, Brigadier-General Anderson established "Camp Dewey," with a battalion of the 1st California Volunteers first making camp there that day. Camp Dewey was 6 miles from Cavite by boat and 21 miles by road. The rainy season was now in full effect. The incessant downpours made life in the cramped American camp particularly miserable.

For the Americans, the situation was rather precarious. The Filipino insurgents had invested Manila and completely dominated the perimeter of the bay. They surrounded not only the Spanish but also the Americans, who clung to a sliver of beach a few miles south of Manila. The only way for US troops to attack Manila was to somehow go through or around the not-entirely friendly insurgents.

On July 17, Brigadier-General Greene's Second Philippine Expedition arrived at Cavite after departing San Francisco on June 15. This second wave of US ground forces comprised 3,600 troops of the 1st Colorado, 1st Nebraska, and 10th Pennsylvania Volunteers, elements of the 18th and 23rd Regular Infantry, and two Utah artillery batteries.

However, the US situation in the Philippines appeared increasingly dicey with each passing day. According to the just-arrived Greene:

> We had been 30 days without news from the outside world. The *Boston* brought us the latest information by way of Hong Kong, which was dated July 2, and consisted of a few brief telegrams... These telegrams showed that a most interesting race was in progress on two sides of the globe, each of the contestants with about 7,000 miles to go. Cámara was coming east, and Merritt was coming west, and the monitor

Monitor USS *Monadnock* crosses the Pacific in the summer of 1898. Its perilously low freeboard was designed to make it a difficult target in coastal waters, but was never intended for deep sea operations. (NHHC NH 60659)

Monterey, which we had left coaling in Honolulu, and was of such vital importance to Dewey, was also coming west, having the same objective – Manila Bay.

Assigning each force a likely speed, Greene calculated that Cámara would reach Manila on July 26, Merritt on July 28, and *Monterey* on August 4. Greene showed his calculations to Dewey, who studied them carefully.

On July 19, Dewey revealed his decision to Greene and Anderson. Dewey knew the safety of the US army and transports so far from home depended on the US fleet remaining intact. If no word was received that Cámara had turned back, then Dewey would take the fleet, including the transports, north of Luzon to cruise east until he had rendezvoused with monitors *Monterey* and *Monadnock* and thus was confident of defeating Cámara. Dewey expected to return to Manila Bay no later than August 10. Brigadier-General Anderson agreed to take 30 days' rations and march his 2,500 men into the hills 20 miles east of Cavite to entrench and await Dewey's return. However, just as Dewey and Anderson were preparing to execute this plan, word came on July 22 that Cámara had turned back to Spain.

Since the siege of Manila began, Aguinaldo had presented surrender terms to Governor-General Augustín three separate times and been refused on all three occasions. Augustín and the Spanish still clung to hope that Spanish reinforcements would arrive, but in late July, Augustín decided that the Spanish position in Manila was hopeless and began negotiations with Aguinaldo. Horrified at the thought of a Spanish governor surrendering Manila without a fight to nonwhite barbarians, Madrid officially relieved the increasingly defeatist and histrionic Augustín on July 24.

The Battle in the Rain, July 31
Meanwhile, the American position slowly continued to strengthen, with the US Army's overall Philippine Expedition commander, Major-General Merritt, arriving at Cavite on July 25. Knowing the Army's Third and Fourth Philippine Expeditions were even now en route to the Philippines, Merritt prepared to seek a decisive engagement. US officers knew Manila was the key to winning the war with Spain, but Manila's entire land perimeter was currently besieged by the Filipino insurgents. Without explicitly acknowledging Aguinaldo's government, the Americans needed to somehow negotiate a section of the Manila front line away from the insurgents to claim for themselves.

Merritt chose Brigadier-General Greene to execute the ruse. Greene promised General Noriel several modern artillery pieces if the Filipinos would withdraw from the lines south of Manila and allow the Americans to take their place. First Noriel and then Aguinaldo were pressured into making an immediate decision. Aguinaldo, perhaps grasping at straws that this was some sort of official recognition, agreed – so long as he got something in writing from Merritt. Greene agreed to get the documentation from Merritt – after the trenches were turned over.

To the dismay of many of his generals, Aguinaldo complied. Exactly why he did so is unclear, as he was already suspicious of American motives. However, Aguinaldo's ability to make un-coerced strategic decisions had evaporated the moment the US government landed ground troops in the Philippines and simultaneously refused to recognize his government. Most

Brigadier General Francis V. Greene in civilian clothes a few years after the 1898 war. Greene's father, General George Sears Greene, had led the Federal defense at Gettysburg's Culp's Hill, while his older brother had been the executive officer of USS *Monitor*, the US Navy's first ironclad warship. (Public domain, via Wikimedia Commons)

Major-General Wesley Merritt in the Philippines. The First, Second, and Third Philippine Expedition convoys had not been the only US Army troops dispatched to the Philippines during the war, but only they arrived in time to see combat against the Spaniards. Meanwhile, the convoys of the Fourth, Fifth, and Sixth Philippines Expeditions would arrive at Manila on August 21, August 24, and August 31, respectively. (NHHC)

likely, Aguinaldo was simply trying to deal with a highly complex and unenviable situation the best he felt he could. Despite Greene's promise, Aguinaldo would never receive any guns or written confirmation from Merritt.

On the night of July 29/30, the Filipino insurgents withdrew from a 1,000-yard section of trench directly facing Fort San Antonio Abad and were replaced by US troops. The trench the Americans took over was occupied by a battalion of the 18th Regulars, a battalion of the 1st Colorado Infantry, and four guns from the two Utah batteries. However, it was shortly afterwards decided to construct a new trench that better commanded the Spanish position, and this would take several days. During this period, the initial American occupants were relieved first by two California infantry battalions, and then, during the morning of July 31, by two battalions of the 10th Pennsylvania Volunteers, one battalion of Nebraska Volunteers, and 200 men of the 3rd Regular Artillery, employed as infantry.

The Americans had not yet admitted to a single combat fatality throughout the entire campaign, and Dewey sincerely believed he could force Manila's surrender and end the war without a single loss of American life. However, the Filipino insurgents relegated to the trenches behind the Americans had by now begun a haphazard behavior of randomly firing over the Americans' heads towards the dug-in Spaniards, who responded in kind. The entrenched Americans were under strict orders to never return fire, but inevitably some did.

Late on the night of July 31, the batteries at Fort San Antonio Abad opened a heavy fire on the Americans during a powerful rainstorm. The entrenched Spanish infantry across no-man's-land also opened a withering fire. Then, on their own initiative, the 10th Pennsylvanians began to advance against the Spanish, claiming dubiously that they were counterattacking a Spanish attempt to turn the American right (eastern) flank. American units in reserve rushed forward to support the Pennsylvanians. Over the next four hours, the advancing Americans and entrenched Spanish enveloped each other in a furious and confused firefight in near- zero visibility. By morning, the "Battle in the Rain" proved something of a draw, with little of consequence won or lost. However, the Americans had lost three killed, their first official combat fatalities of the campaign.

The following night, August 1, the Colorado Volunteers held the line. The Americans were again under strict orders not to return fire unless the Spanish were advancing from their trenches. This was not entirely obeyed, and in the potshots that followed one American was killed and four wounded. By August 4, the Americans had lost 12 killed and 54 wounded in these incidents. The following night, August 5, saw yet another skirmish erupt under the usual pretext that "the Spanish were advancing." After three hours of shooting, the Americans had lost another three dead and seven wounded.

The Battle in the Rain, July 31/August 1, 1898

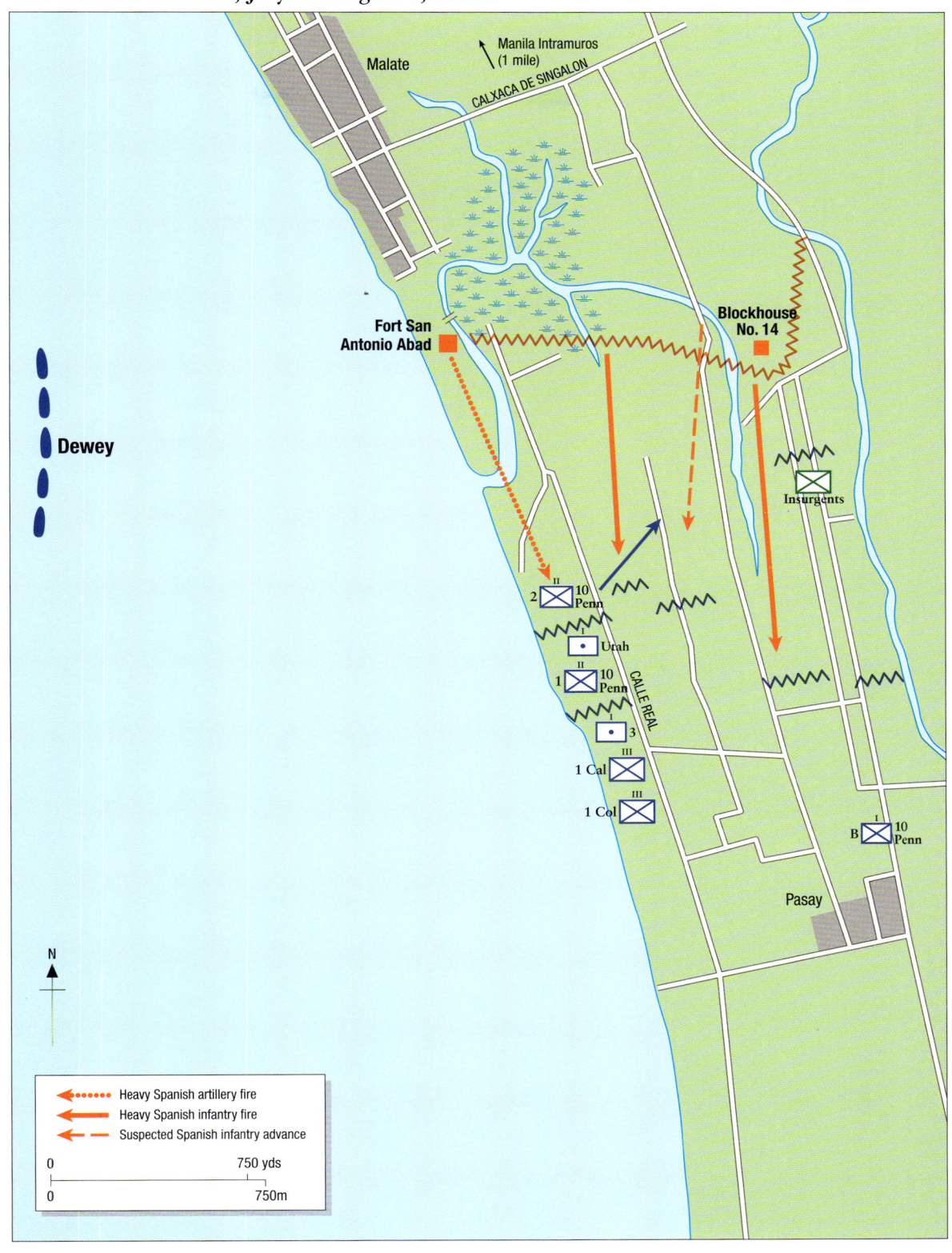

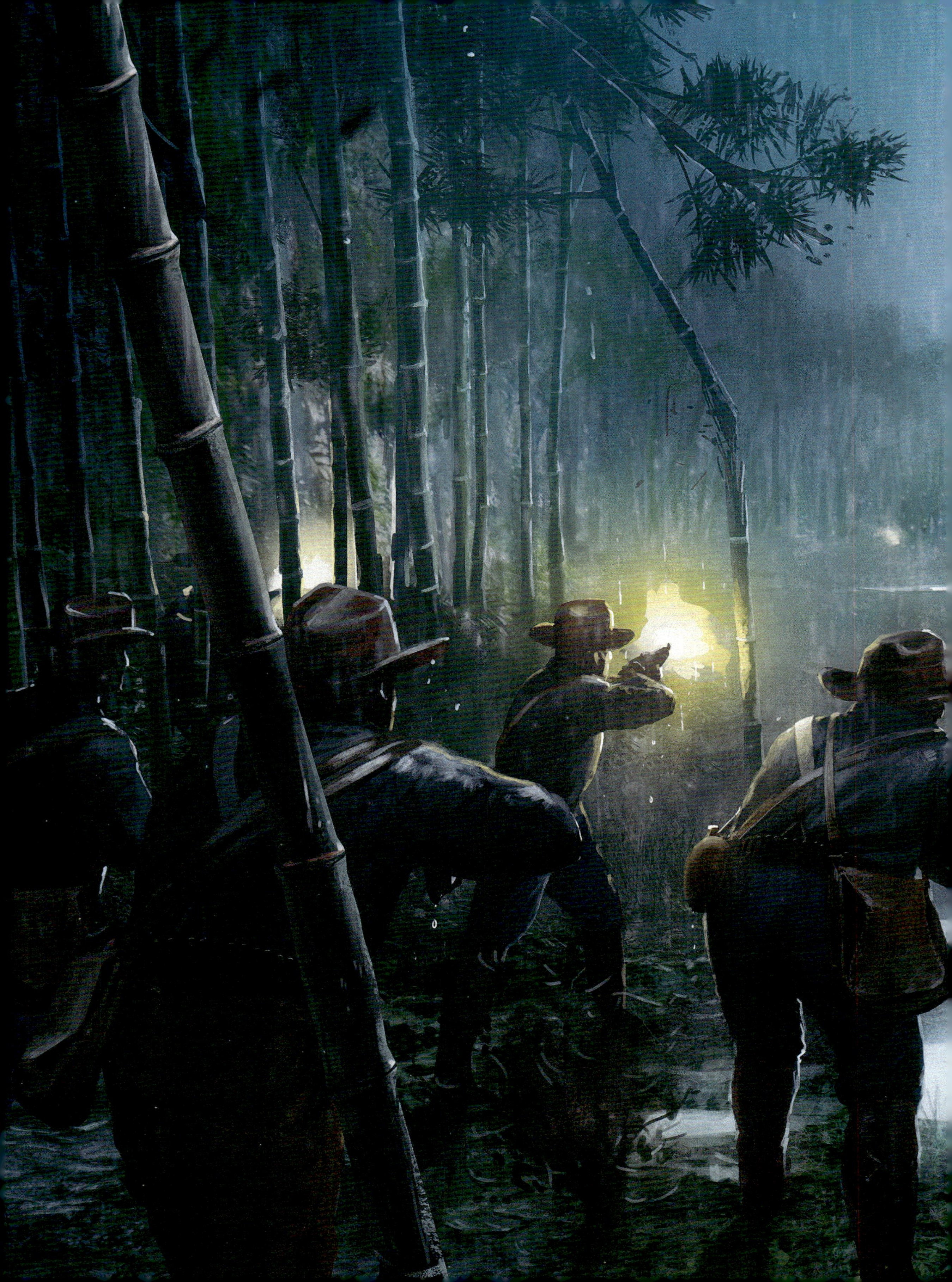

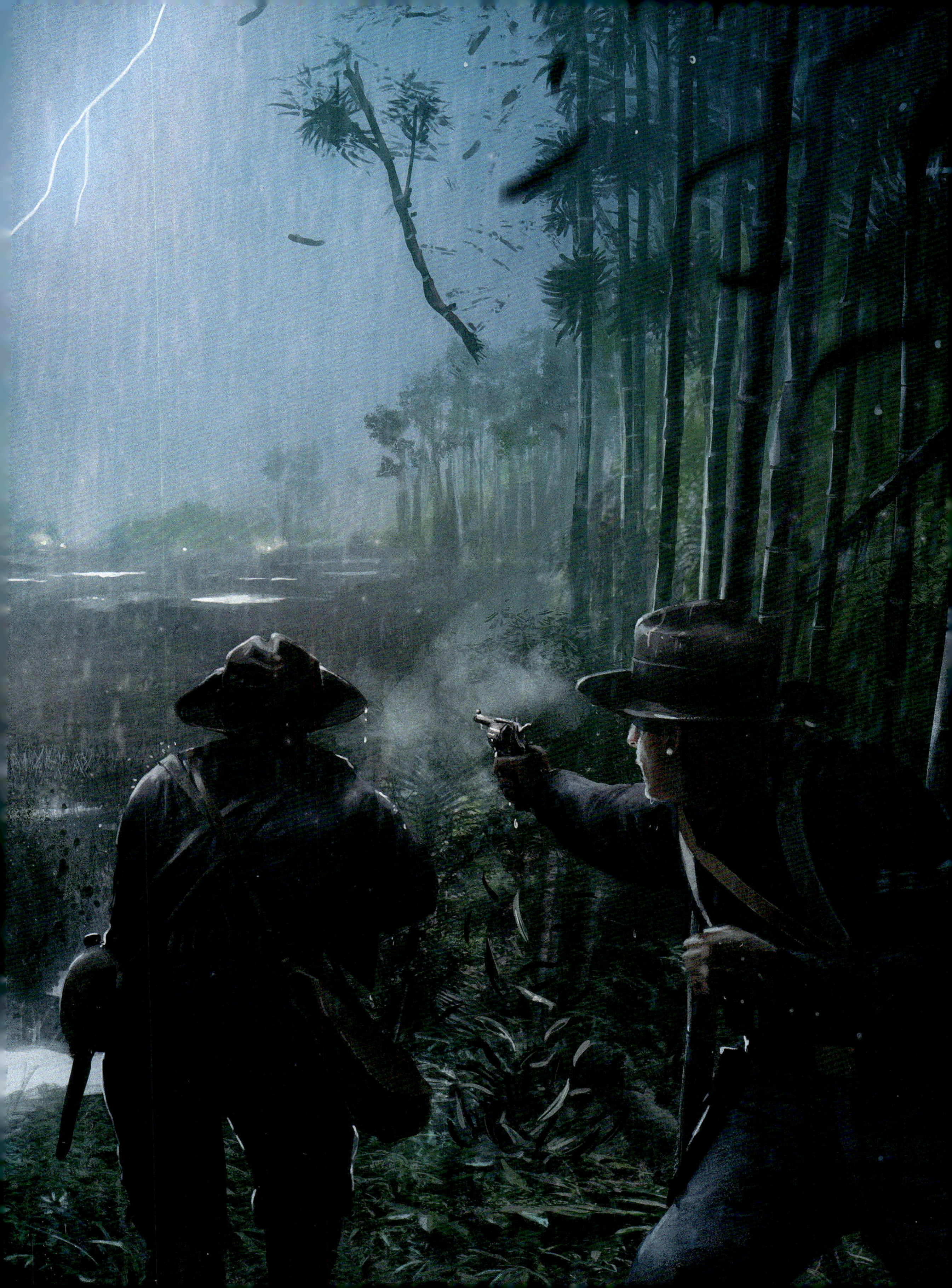

THE BATTLE IN THE RAIN, JULY 31/AUGUST 1, 1898 (PP. 78–79)

A furious tropical storm raged over Manila the night of July 31. The severe downpour and high winds reduced visibility to mere yards. Suddenly, around 2230hrs, four Spanish guns at Fort San Antonio Abad opened a heavy artillery barrage at the American front, accompanied by intense rifle fire from entrenched Spanish infantry across from the Americans **(1)**.

The Spanish line extended well beyond the US right. The 10th Pennsylvania Regiment was holding the front of the American line, and the resulting enfilading Spanish fire caused the Pennsylvanians to report that the Spanish were attacking and attempting to turn the American right. The 3rd Artillery moved forward to counterattack, as did the 1st California and 1st Colorado Infantry **(2)**.

With the Spanish typically firing high, a "perfect maelstrom of firing" extended from the front of the American lines to 700 yards in the rear. The provoked Americans returned fire over the next four hours, expending 60,000 rifle rounds into the Spanish positions, about half the rounds believed fired from the Spanish lines. Spanish artillery kept up its own bombardment, and this claimed the first American casualty, when Pennsylvania's Lieutenant Buttermore was struck across the eyes by a shell fragment. Buttermore nevertheless recovered and continued to fight. Shortly afterwards, however, the Pennsylvanians' Corporal N. E. Brown of Company D was killed by Spanish fire, becoming the US's first official combat death of the campaign. The focus of the Spanish fire, the front American trenches, was already overcrowded with defenders. Even so, Major Boxtun's battalion of 1st California Volunteers charged forward into heavy fire to reinforce the front lines. Its Company D commander, Captain Reinhold Richter, was the first Californian to fall – from a shot to the head. Shortly afterwards, 1st Sergeant Maurice Justh of Company A took a shot through his body, killing him instantly. As the Californians charged forward, they came upon gun flashes at point blank range. Assuming them to be Spaniards, the Californians fired three full volleys at short range into what turned out to be the 10th Pennsylvanians and the Regulars. Colonel Smith of the Californians realized the mistake and sent a message back to Major Boxtun clarifying the situation. It is here that the official details become suspicious, as the surgeon on the scene later claimed not a single American had been killed by a shot fired from the rear.

Once the Californians reached the front and order was restored, they took over from the hard-fought Pennsylvanians. Meanwhile, the cruiser *Boston* was anchored in a position to take the whole Spanish trench, but Dewey feared friendly casualties and ordered *Boston* to stand down except as a last resort. As Brigadier-General Greene studied the Spanish fire, he became convinced the Spanish were still in their trenches and not attacking, as the American reports stated. Greene therefore chose not to signal *Boston* for fire support. After 3–4 hours of Spanish bombardment and American return fire, the fighting died down, having produced no real changes on the battlefield.

Dewey and Merritt now announced to the Spaniards that if such attacks did not cease, a general land and naval attack would commence against Manila in 48 hours, explaining that the notice was given so that women, children, and other noncombatants could be removed from the city. This immediately ended all attacks by the Spanish until the final assault on the capital.

On August 6, Aguinaldo issued a memorandum to the various great powers, in which he announced he had 9,000 prisoners of war and that his Filipino government was treating the prisoners "with the same consideration observed by cultured nations, agreeably with the sentiments of humanity," and also announced that his Revolutionary army had a "regularly organized army of more than 30,000 men fully equipped on a war footing."

In addition to the memorandum, Aguinaldo issued copies of the Philippine Declaration of Independence. According to contemporary historian John Foreman: "The result was altogether negative. Not a single Power chose to embarrass America, especially at that critical period, by a recognition of Aguinaldo's party."

Merritt later admitted in his report that Aguinaldo had "proclaimed an independent government, republican in form, with himself as President, and at the time of my arrival in the Islands the entire edifice of executive and legislative departments had been accomplished, at least on paper."

"Of course," James H. Blount stated in his own contemporary history, "at that time we were still officially declining to take Filipino aspirations for independence seriously and preferred to treat Aguinaldo's government as purely a matter of stationery."

Back on August 4, Augustín's replacement, Fermín Jáudenes, had taken over command of the Manila garrison. On August 7, sensing an opportunity, Dewey and Merritt sent the first in a series of flowery and magnanimous Victorian-era-style correspondences to Jáudenes informing the new governor-general that Manila had 48 hours to either surrender or evacuate its noncombatants before the Americans launched a full-scale attack on the city. Using the same flowery, magnanimous tone, Jáudenes cheekily responded that he would allow the Americans to attack, should they feel it necessary. On August 8, Dewey and Merritt repeated their request to Jáudenes to surrender, but this time even more politely. Jáudenes graciously acknowledged Manila's predicament but, preferring to stall, requested time to consult the Madrid government via Hong Kong. This was again respectfully denied by the Americans.

By August 10, the Americans were preparing to assault Manila. The seven ships and 4,800 troops of the US Third Philippine Expedition had arrived at Cavite on July 31, under the command of Brigadier-General Arthur MacArthur, and they were now fully deployed in the field. MacArthur's force included the remaining elements of the 18th and 23rd Regular Infantry, a company of engineers, a battalion of the 3rd Regular Artillery, plus the 1st North Dakota, 1st Idaho, and 13th Minnesota Volunteers, a battalion from the 1st Wyoming, and the Astor Battery of artillery.

The flag of the Revolutionary Government of the Philippines in 1898. After the battle of Alapan, Aguinaldo marched his troops to Cavite and unfurled the new flag for the first time. The Revolutionary Government was itself replaced on January 23, 1899 by the First Republic of the Philippines. Neither government was ever recognized by other powers. (Public domain, via Wikimedia Commons)

Brigadier-General Arthur MacArthur, Jr. commanded the US 1st Brigade. An outstanding officer in his own right, MacArthur was also the father of future US general and Philippines governor/field marshal Douglas MacArthur. Both were heavily associated with the Philippines and would become the first father–son pair to be awarded Medals of Honor. (User:Magalhães, public domain, via Wikimedia Commons)

Spain's last governor-general of the Philippines, Fermín Jáudenes. He was the Philippines' sixth governor-general or acting governor-general in less than a two-year period, an indication of the Manila government's dire military and political situation. (Public domain, via Wikimedia Commons)

Now wielding a larger, more complete force, Major-General Merritt had reorganized the US troops in the Philippines as the 2nd Division of the Eighth Army Corps, with Brigadier-General Anderson commanding the division. The 2nd Division was divided into the 1st Brigade under Brigadier-General Arthur MacArthur and the 2nd Brigade under Brigadier-General Francis V. Greene.

Additionally, monitor USS *Monterey* and accompanying collier *Brutus* had reached the Philippines on August 4; *Monterey*'s two 12in and two 10in cannon had abruptly become the most powerful battery in Manila Bay by a wide margin. *Monterey* greatly increased Dewey's available naval firepower, and he immediately incorporated the monitor into his plans to capture Manila.

Brigadier-General Anderson now moved his headquarters from Cavite to the Manila siege lines to take formal divisional command. The brigade commanders both urged that US troops should occupy the strongest insurgent trenches, whether through persuasion or force. However, Merritt specifically forbade any words or action that might offend the insurgents.

THE BATTLE OF MANILA, AUGUST 13

By August 1898, Manila's walled inner city Intramuros, a quarter of a square mile and normally with a population of 10,000 residents, had swelled to 70,000 residents, making living conditions "unbearable." The Spanish position had long been hopeless. With the fall of Manila inevitable, both the US and Spanish commands in the Philippines increasingly desired that Manila's capitulation be as bloodless and honorable as possible.

Fortunately, Dewey remained in covert contact with Jáudenes through a Belgian consul, Edouard C. André. Via André, Jáudenes hinted on August 10 that he might surrender Manila to the Americans after a face-saving sham battle, provided the insurgents were kept out of the city. Dewey indicated that he agreed, then publicly announced that an attack on Manila would begin in 48 hours and advised all foreign warships to remove themselves from the line of fire and anchor at Cavite – all but von Diederichs' German squadron complied.

By August 12, full details of the mock battle had been secretly hammered out between Dewey, Merritt, and Governor-General Jáudenes. Even by 19th-century standards, the scheme was breathtaking in its political audacity and casual racism:

1. The Americans were to make such a display of firepower that any third-party observer would consider Spanish defiance useless, and thus satisfy Spanish cultural requirements to surrender.
2. However, no lives on either side were to be taken or endangered.
3. The Spanish would explicitly surrender Manila to the Americans only.
4. In accepting the Spanish surrender, the Americans would actively shut Aguinaldo's Filipinos out of Manila, the insurgents' own capital.
5. The insurgents – the Americans' erstwhile quasi-allies – were to know nothing of the secret Spanish–American plan.

Each of the plan's first four points would be difficult enough to coordinate on their own merits. However, the final point alone threatened to demolish the entire scheme single-handedly.

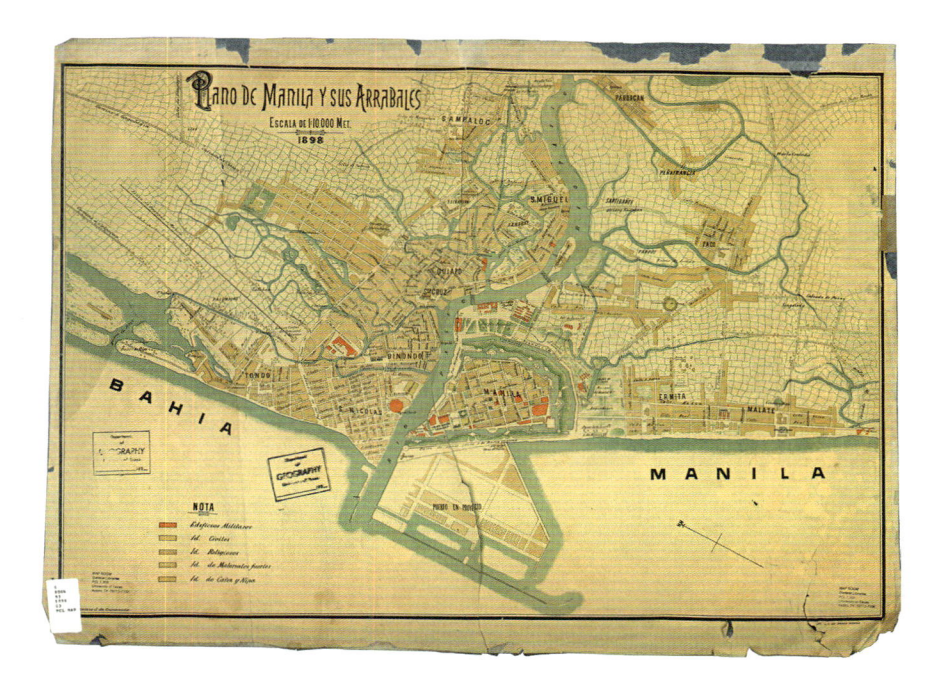

A Spanish map of Manila and suburbs. Manila had once been the western end of the prosperous Manila galleon trade with New Spain (Mexico), but by August 1898, Manila was Spain's last major Pacific possession still holding out. (Franciso J. de Gamoneda, public domain, via Wikimedia Commons)

Indeed, the insurgents were in a much stronger position than the Americans accepted. Manila's continued economic life depended on trade with the rest of Luzon, which only existed with the consent of the besieging insurgents. Aguinaldo's men were also in control of the city waterworks, a fact the US command did acknowledge as a dangerous liability. While not informed of the plan, the insurgents had divined the Spanish–American conspiracy and even the time of the assault – the next morning, August 13. Aguinaldo thus planned to force his command into the proceedings unilaterally.

The exact deployment of forces and timing and method of events were planned ahead of time and shared only between both sides' high commands. These included the planned maneuvers of Dewey's squadron; when and how the Americans would open fire (on the evacuated Fort San Antonio Abad); that the Spanish would not fire back; and the exact time and method of Spanish surrender.

However, late on August 12, there would be one last unscripted battle. That night, Spanish troops charged the outnumbered American lines, but a counterattack by the Americans drove the Spaniards out of the first Spanish trench line 350 yards away. This was met with a furious Spanish bayonet charge that in turn drove the Americans out of both the Spanish trench and the first US trench line, forcing the Americans to abandon four artillery pieces. A final counterattack, this time by the Filipino insurgents behind the Americans, recovered the American trench and the guns.

At 0900hrs on August 13, Dewey began deploying his fleet for the "attack." By now, Dewey's fleet was considerably more powerful than the plucky squadron that had pried its way into Manila Bay three months earlier. At 0930hrs, *Olympia* was in position to bombard Fort San Antonio Abad. Off *Olympia*'s port quarter were *Boston*, *Charleston*, and *Baltimore*, and off the flagship's starboard quarter was *McCulloch*. Behind *Olympia* were *Raleigh* and *Petrel*, with the small captured Spanish gunboats *Callao* and *Barcelo* deployed further landwards with the monitor *Monterey*, whose

Protected cruiser USS *Charleston* at Manila in 1898. *Charleston* was one of two major naval reinforcements Dewey received before the fall of Manila, the other being the monitor *Monterey*. *Charleston* would spend the rest of its brief career in the Philippines supporting the US counterinsurgency. It was wrecked off Luzon in 1899, becoming the first Steel Navy warship to be lost in service. (Collection of Rear Admiral Ammen Farenholt, NHHC NH 55084)

"12-inch muzzles stood grinning at the heavy Krupp batteries at the Luneta." Behind these vessels was the troopship *Newport* hosting Major-General Merritt and his staff, and the steamer *Kwonghai* carrying the Oregon troops whom Merritt hoped to land directly in the Intramuros immediately after the scripted ceasefire. To the north stood *Concord* at the mouth of the Pasig. According to Faust: "The threatening array would have amply justified the Spanish surrender without a shot, but the play went on, with the head of the army and escort in the rear, waiting for the white flag and the peals of victory [signaling] the capitulation of the city as per arrangement."

Meanwhile, Merritt had scripted the US Army's part of the fraud, but the day's events made clear he informed few subordinates of the conspiracy itself. Merritt merely announced that a naval and artillery attack was to begin on the morning of August 13, and that the American troops were strictly to hold their trenches and "make no advance." MacArthur's 1st Brigade, with eight battalions in line and three in reserve, was to hold the right of the line on the Manila–Pasai road, but "have for its immediate objective the Spanish blockhouse No. 14 and adjoining trenches." Greene's 2nd Brigade, with three of its battalions in line and eight in reserve, was to hold the left of the line, operating along the beaches and adjoining trenches. The reserve battalions of both brigades were to assemble in an open field to the west of the Camino Real road, where they fell under the personal command of the 2nd Division commander, Major-General Anderson.

Merritt was in fact privately skeptical that any sham battle could in any way be controlled, fearing clashes with insurgents and suspecting some Spaniards would fight to the death. Merritt prepared as if a real battle might take place, equipping his men with several days' rations and 200 rounds of ammunition each, as well as heavy spades, axes, and hatchets for each four-man section, all of which furthered the masquerade that a real assault was imminent. Merritt summed up his instructions: "All positions should be taken up by 9 A. M., the 13th… Our line will not advance except under orders of the general in the field."

At 0930hrs, Dewey's warships opened the charade bombardment. Dewey had only told four of his captains the bombardment was fake. Allegedly, the gunners of at least one ship – perhaps *Olympia* itself – noticed they had been given bad targeting information, assumed it was a mistake, corrected the range, and did such obvious damage that their captain withdrew from the battle entirely. According to additional lore, as the shelling began, von Diederichs' German cruisers formed to steam across Dewey's advancing squadron, but Captain Chichester's HMS *Immortalité* charged out from Cavite and pulled in front of the Germans, with Chichester later explaining "Blood is thicker than water." While foreign ships did scramble to get a better view, nothing more deliberate was recorded at the time, and the entire story may be retroactive World War I propaganda.

However, immediately prior to the bombardment, Merritt had ordered Greene to advance a regiment as soon as the shelling had demonstrated an effect. Without waiting for Dewey's planned signal requesting surrender, Greene sent the 1st Colorado Volunteers forward, advancing in front of the trenches in an open field and along the beach, in wide view of the Spanish defenders in the woods behind the abandoned Fort San Antonio Abad. The startled Spaniards opened fire at what appeared to be a breach of the agreement. Led by a Lieutenant-Colonel McCoy, the Coloradoans continued to advance under fire, wading up the beach and taking the unoccupied fort. They hauled down the Spanish flag and ran up the Stars and Stripes, prompting cheers from the Americans. It was at this moment that the Coloradoans' color bearer was shot. Greene's Coloradoans, however, continued to push forward into the town of Malate.

A US soldier points out a shell hole in Fort San Antonio Abad after the August 13 bombardment. The hole may have been created by the 6in *Olympia* shell that detonated the fort's magazine. (Donation of C. J. Dutreaux, NHHC USN 902954)

On the right, MacArthur's 1st Brigade was out of view of Dewey's fleet, but once MacArthur saw the US flag raised over Fort San Antonio Abad, he ordered the 1st Brigade to attack Blockhouse No. 14. The Utah and Astor batteries quickly turned the strongpoint to rubble, but the Spaniards continued to resist.

At 1025hrs, on schedule, Dewey had finished his "bombardment" of Fort San Antonio Abad. He steamed *Olympia* north until he was 2 miles off Manila's Paseo de Luneta waterfront. At 1100hrs, *Olympia* duly hoisted "DWHB," the international signal meaning, "Do you surrender?" Only after several long moments and much anxiety did Dewey himself spy the white flag hanging over a southern wall of the Luneta. Nevertheless, US troops continued to advance, most likely not understanding the battle was supposed to be over. MacArthur's 1st Brigade would not capture Blockhouse No. 14 until 1120hrs, 20 minutes after the surrender.

However, the Americans and Spanish now had an unscripted crisis to deal with. At 0800hrs that morning, Anderson had telegraphed Aguinaldo that the Americans would attack Manila without insurgent help and that Aguinaldo's command should be kept outside the city. "Too late," was Aguinaldo's laconic response. Understanding the gig was finally up, Aguinaldo had sent in 4,000 of General Noriel's men behind MacArthur's and Greene's advancing US troops – despite Dewey having earlier threatened to bombard the Filipinos with the gunboat *Petrel* should they advance.

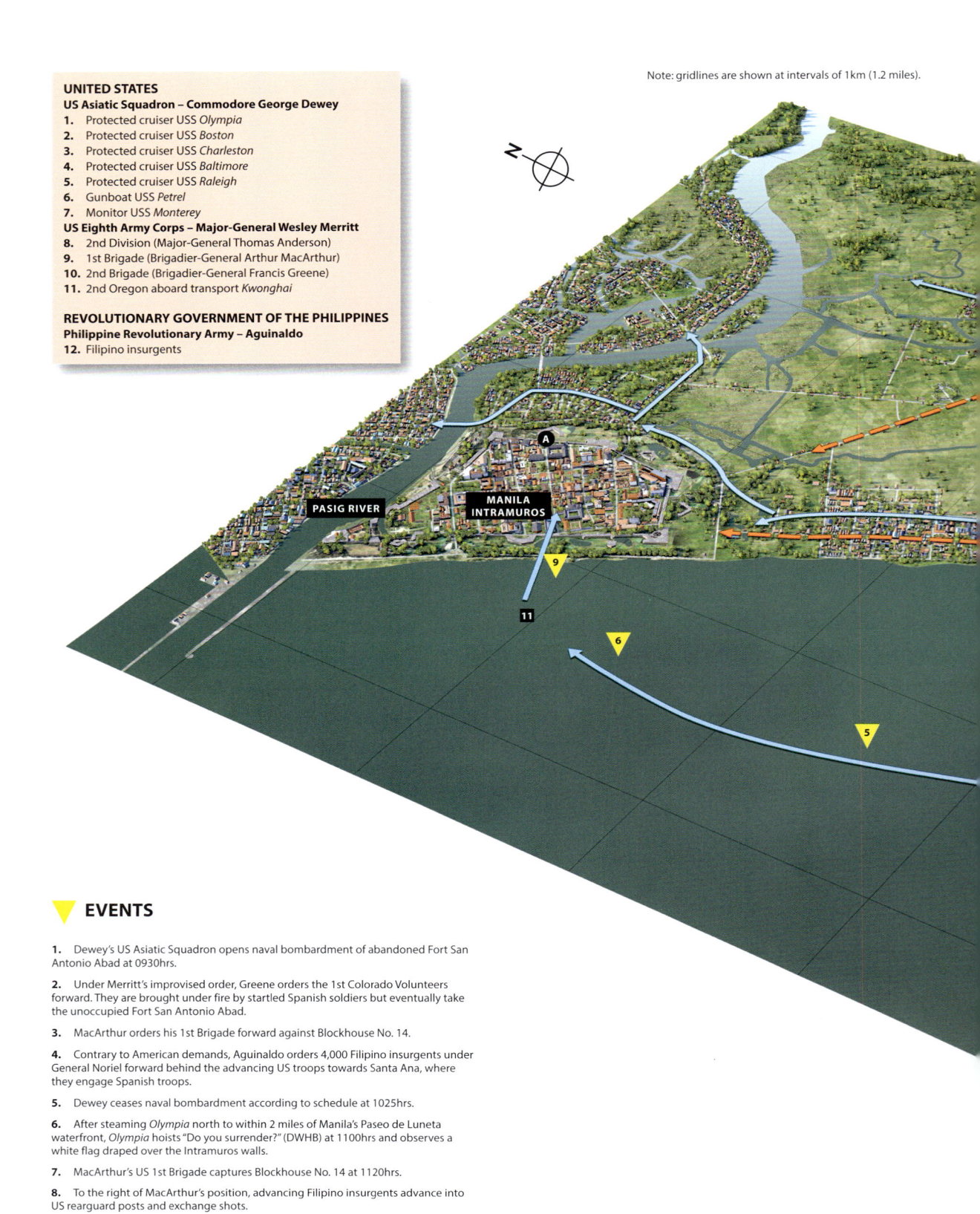

Note: gridlines are shown at intervals of 1km (1.2 miles).

UNITED STATES
US Asiatic Squadron – Commodore George Dewey
1. Protected cruiser USS *Olympia*
2. Protected cruiser USS *Boston*
3. Protected cruiser USS *Charleston*
4. Protected cruiser USS *Baltimore*
5. Protected cruiser USS *Raleigh*
6. Gunboat USS *Petrel*
7. Monitor USS *Monterey*

US Eighth Army Corps – Major-General Wesley Merritt
8. 2nd Division (Major-General Thomas Anderson)
9. 1st Brigade (Brigadier-General Arthur MacArthur)
10. 2nd Brigade (Brigadier-General Francis Greene)
11. 2nd Oregon aboard transport *Kwonghai*

REVOLUTIONARY GOVERNMENT OF THE PHILIPPINES
Philippine Revolutionary Army – Aguinaldo
12. Filipino insurgents

PASIG RIVER

MANILA INTRAMUROS

▼ EVENTS

1. Dewey's US Asiatic Squadron opens naval bombardment of abandoned Fort San Antonio Abad at 0930hrs.

2. Under Merritt's improvised order, Greene orders the 1st Colorado Volunteers forward. They are brought under fire by startled Spanish soldiers but eventually take the unoccupied Fort San Antonio Abad.

3. MacArthur orders his 1st Brigade forward against Blockhouse No. 14.

4. Contrary to American demands, Aguinaldo orders 4,000 Filipino insurgents under General Noriel forward behind the advancing US troops towards Santa Ana, where they engage Spanish troops.

5. Dewey ceases naval bombardment according to schedule at 1025hrs.

6. After steaming *Olympia* north to within 2 miles of Manila's Paseo de Luneta waterfront, *Olympia* hoists "Do you surrender?" (DWHB) at 1100hrs and observes a white flag draped over the Intramuros walls.

7. MacArthur's US 1st Brigade captures Blockhouse No. 14 at 1120hrs.

8. To the right of MacArthur's position, advancing Filipino insurgents advance into US rearguard posts and exchange shots.

9. Merritt lands the 2nd Oregon directly into the Intramuros from transport *Kwonghai*, where they raise the US flag at 1750hrs.

THE BATTLE OF MANILA, AUGUST 13, 1898

The planned "mock" battle of Manila inevitably breaks down in a real three-way battle that ultimately results in US control of the Intramuros.

SPAIN
Ejército de Tierra – Governor-General Fermín Jáudenes y Álvarez
A. Defending Spanish troops

Troops of the 1st Colorado Volunteers pose after capturing the battered Fort San Antonio Abad on August 13, 1898. It is unlikely any of them understood the fort had already been abandoned by agreement when they attacked it. (Donation of Rear Admiral Ammen C. Farenholt, NHHC NH 43149)

Sailors prepare to raise *Olympia*'s American flag over Manila on the afternoon of August 13, 1898. *Olympia*'s Lieutenant Ellicott stated, "I had a curious feeling that it was almost a sacrilege to cause those beautiful flags of a 400-year-old nation to flutter down in defeat." (Estate of Lieutenant C. J. Dutreaux, NHHC WHI.2014.37)

As the Filipino insurgents approached Santa Ana, they ran into Spanish troops, causing a fierce skirmish to erupt. Then, on the right of MacArthur's 1st Brigade, insurgents ran into US rearguard posts deployed to block the Filipino advance, and shots were exchanged.

Meanwhile, Dewey and Merritt had already sent two US officers ashore to negotiate terms. By 1430hrs, they signaled success to Dewey's fleet. Merritt immediately landed to sign a preliminary agreement with Jáudenes, while the 2nd Oregon landed to secure the Intramuros. Finally, at 1750hrs on August 13, the last Spanish flag was hauled down over Manila and *Olympia*'s largest US ensign run up in its place. Each of Dewey's ships fired a 21-gun salute, followed by HMS *Immortalité*, flying the Stars and Stripes from its mainmast. "It was a most dramatic scene," Dewey's flag lieutenant recalled. "An empire had changed hands."

At least six Americans and 49 Spaniards had been killed in the "mock battle of Manila." US forces would take the surrender of 5,600 Spanish troops in Manila, plus 22,000 small arms. In addition to the Manila surrender, Spanish troops in the Philippines had suffered about 1,000 killed or mortally wounded in combat; 2,600 were wounded or diseased in Manila hospitals; 8,000 were prisoners to the Filipino rebels; 1,000 were detached in the Luzon provinces and were subsequently killed or captured by the rebels; and about 3,000 were still stationed in the Visayas and Mindanao under Rios. The Americans, in contrast, had lost about 20 men killed and less than 150 wounded during the entire Philippines campaign.

However, the unpleasantness was not over with the Spanish capitulation. Quite unknown to anyone in the Philippines, on August 12 – the day before the final battle in Manila – the governments of Spain

The American flag flies over Manila's captured Fort Santiago on August 13, 1898 in this contemporary illustration in *Harper's Weekly*. Unlike Fort San Antonio Abad, which lay just to the south, Fort Santiago was part of the Intramuros itself. (George W. Peters, public domain, via Wikimedia Commons)

and the United States had agreed on a global ceasefire. The Washington, DC, conference stipulated "That the United States will occupy and hold the city, bay, and harbor of Manila, pending the conclusion of a treaty of peace, which shall determine the control, disposition, and government of the Philippines."

Yet the Filipino insurgents badly wanted to occupy their ancient capital they had done so much to liberate. Many attempted to infiltrate past the US troops, who were ordered to arrest and disarm them. With admirable restraint, Aguinaldo set up a group of commissioners to meet with US officials and negotiate. With victors' magnanimity, Merritt, Anderson, and Dewey received the commission and even made a few concessions – permitting the insurgents to keep some of their gains near Manila, returning captured insurgent weapons, and allowing Filipino officers into Manila, even with sidearms.

However, the delicate balance could not survive forever. A large, well-armed, and battle-hardened Filipino army watched frustrated and restless just outside its abruptly stolen main objective, while even more troop-laden convoys were en route to reinforce the Americans. By August 13 – the day of Manila's capitulation – an increasingly nervous Merritt telegraphed Washington:

> Since occupation of town and suburbs the insurgents on the outside are pressing demand for joint occupation of city. Situation difficult… Inform me at once how far I shall proceed in forcing this matter and others that may arise. Is government willing to use all means to make natives submit to the authority of the United States?

Merritt received the following reply from Washington:

> The President directs that there must be no joint occupation of the insurgents. The United States… must preserve the peace… The insurgents and all others must recognize the military occupation and authority of the United States. Use whatever means, in your judgment, is necessary to this end…

AFTERMATH

The United States and the Kingdom of Spain signed the Treaty of Paris on December 10, 1898. Among its many provisions was that Spain would sell the Philippines and Guam to the United States for $20 million. The US Congress ratified the treaty on February 6, 1899, formally ending the Spanish–American War. For a relatively small war, the 1898 Philippine campaign had huge ramifications.

SPAIN

The final destruction of the Spanish Empire left deep psychological scars on the Spanish people. An entire national movement – the "Generation of '98" – arose dedicated to reforming Spanish society through artistic and literary criticism. Spanish political connection to the West was virtually suspended through most of the 20th century – Spain sat out both world wars, was ruled for 40 years by a semi-fascist dictatorship, and only joined NATO in 1978.

More immediately, Spain sold the Northern Marianas to Imperial Germany in 1899, a move that had massive effects for the future. Those German islands were conquered by Japan in 1914, and in World War II provided Japan's main line of defense against advancing US forces.

THE UNITED STATES

On the American side, the "splendid little war" was the herald of a new American overseas empire. Not only were the Philippines, Guam, and Puerto Rico annexed as spoils of victory, but US expansion into the Pacific continued. On January 17, 1899, gunboat USS *Bennington* formally claimed unoccupied Wake Island for the United States. Then on February 19, 1900, President McKinley formally annexed the eastern Samoa islands, now called American Samoa. Two months later, on April 30, 1900, the US government established Hawai'i as an organized and incorporated US territory, making the new Territory of Hawaii a legal and inseparable part of the US homeland.

Between 1899 and 1909, a frenzied US naval program would build 21 new battleships and ten new armored cruisers, suddenly making the US Navy the world's second-largest. The linchpin of the new American empire was the US-operated Panama Canal, built between 1904 and 1914 to facilitate the transoceanic transfer of US naval and commercial shipping.

American public reaction to the new empire was mixed, with the famous Anti-Imperialist League formed as early as June 15, 1898 to protest that unilateral territorial acquisitions were hypocritical to traditional American values of self-determination. Among the League's prominent members were Grover Cleveland, Andrew Carnegie, and Mark Twain. However, within ten years, the anti-imperialists had largely lost the battle of public opinion to the political and commercial elites.

Ultimately, US possession of the Philippines would lead directly to Japan's decision to attack the United States in 1941. Therefore, without the United States' 1898 conquest of the Philippines, 20th-century history would have taken a drastically different path.

The official August 23, 1898 annexation ceremony of Hawaii. The Hawaiian flag is being lowered at the Iolani Palace in Honolulu. Moments later, the US flag would be raised in its place. Over a century later, the issue of Hawaiian sovereignty remains a contentious state issue. (Frank Davey, public domain, via Wikimedia Commons)

THE PHILIPPINES

As the United States unilaterally imposed its own rule on the Philippines, the Filipinos realized they had merely exchanged one white master for another. On February 4, 1899, a US soldier fatally shot a Filipino who had been mocking him, sparking the long-inevitable showdown. The resulting Philippine–American War proved far more vicious and deadly than the Spanish–American War, killing over 4,000 Americans and 200,000 Filipinos. It was also one of the most decisive counterinsurgency victories in modern history, capped with a dramatic American capture of Aguinaldo in 1901 that essentially decided the conflict.

Uncle Sam can't let go of the Philippines in this political cartoon from the November 23, 1898 issue of the satirical *Puck* magazine. Threatening the Filipina maiden are two tigers – the tiger on the left is labeled "Spanish misrule" and the one on the right is labeled "Aguinaldoism." (Louis Dalrymple, published by Keppler & Schwarzmann November 23, 1898, LOC Prints and Photographs Division)

In hindsight, an independent, self-governing, Aguinaldo-led Philippines under the guidance and protection of the United States – that conceded a long-term lease of Subic Bay to the US government as a semi-sovereign naval and trading port – would probably have solved the major problems for both countries. While not perfect, similar situations such as Hong Kong, Guantanamo Bay, and the Panama Canal all survived the 20th century with relatively little disruption, while their host countries, implicitly protected by superpowers, largely modernized around them.

On July 1, 1902, the United States established the Insular Government of the Philippines, whose executive and upper legislative house were appointed by the US government, but whose lower house was directly elected by Filipinos. Finally, on March 24, 1934, the US Congress passed the Tydings-McDuffie Act, which established a ten-year process for the Philippines to assume independence from the United States. Authorized elections and a new constitution established the semi-autonomous Commonwealth of the Philippines in 1935. The schedule was interrupted by Japan's December 1941 invasion, which finally crushed the last organized American and Filipino resistance in May 1942. After a brutal Japanese occupation, US forces returned in October 1944 to liberate the Philippines, with the last Japanese troops in Luzon surrendering in August 1945. On July 4, 1946, the Philippines finally celebrated its long-awaited independence.

THE BATTLEFIELD TODAY

Much of 1898-era Manila was destroyed during the 1945 battle of Manila. However, some buildings have survived to the present day, mostly in the quarter-square-mile Intramuros. Since 1979, the Intramuros has been cared for by the Intramuros Administration, a section of the Philippines Department of Tourism charged with preserving Spanish–Philippine heritage within the district. Nearby Fort San Antonio Abad was also heavily damaged during World War II and was only restored in the 1970s. It is currently a part of the Bangko Sentral ng Pilipinas (Central Bank of the Philippines) complex.

Some relics of Montojo's destroyed squadron survive. Four of *Reina Cristina*'s 3-pdr guns guard the US Coast Guard Academy grounds in New London, Connecticut. Two 5.9in cannon from *Castilla* are on display at the Vermont Statehouse, and a third resides at Highland Park in Rochester, New York. Both of *Boston*'s 8in guns have been preserved at Hamlin Park in Shoreline, Washington. Two 6in guns from *Concord* survive on display at the Veterans' Memorial Museum in Chehalis, Washington.

Dewey's flagship USS *Olympia* survives as a museum ship in Philadelphia. The cruiser is currently the ward of the Independence Seaport Museum and berthed at Penn's Landing on the Delaware River. *Olympia* is the last surviving warship from the 1898 Spanish–American War and one of the few surviving steel-hulled steamships from the 19th century anywhere in the world.

Since its Spanish–American War service, much of the cruiser had either been heavily modified, stripped of items, or simply deteriorated. It would take decades for volunteers and the necessary funding to slowly refurbish *Olympia* and largely return it to its 1898 appearance. This includes steel mock-ups of *Olympia*'s long-removed 8in twin turrets and many 5in rapid-firing guns cannibalized from other vessels that were being scrapped.

Much of the ship is open for tours. Naval fans can visit *Olympia*'s armored conning tower, with its helm and cramped space for just one man – the captain. But surely the highlight of the preserved *Olympia* is one deck directly above the conning tower. Here on the open bridge, one can stand exactly where Dewey conducted the battle and issued his immortal command, "You may fire when you are ready, Gridley."

SELECT BIBLIOGRAPHY

Action Reports of various US and Spanish officers (1898)
Blount, James H., *The American Occupation of the Philippines 1898–1912*, New York and London: G. P. Putnam's Sons, Knickerbocker Press (1913)
Burr, Lawrence, *US Cruisers 1883–1904*, Oxford: Osprey Publishing (2008)
De Quesada, Alejandro, *The Spanish-American War and Philippine Insurrection*, Oxford: Osprey Publishing (2007)
Ellicott, Captain J. M., "Cold War Between Von Diederichs and Dewey in Manila Bay" in *Proceedings*, Vol. 81/11/633 (November 1955)
Faust, Karl Irving, *Campaigning in the Philippines*, San Francisco, CA: Hicks-Judd Company Publishers (1899)
Franklin, Colling B., *USS Olympia: Herald of Empire*, Annapolis, MD: Naval Institute Press (2007)
Foreman, John, F.R.G.S., *The Philippine Islands. A Political, Geographical, Ethnographical, Social and Commercial History of the Philippine Archipelago and its Political Dependencies, Embracing the Whole Period of Spanish Rule*, New York: C. Scribner's Sons (1899)
Halstead, Murat, *The Story of the Philippines and Our New Possessions, Including The Ladrones, Hawaii, Cuba and Porto Rico*, Chicago: Our Possessions Publishing Co. (1898)
Herder, Brian Lane, *US Navy Battleships 1886–98: The pre-dreadnoughts and monitors that fought the Spanish-American War*, Oxford: Osprey Publishing (2019)
Herder, Brian Lane, *US Navy Battleships 1895–1908: The Great White Fleet and the beginning of US global naval power*, Oxford: Osprey Publishing (2020)
Herder, Brian Lane, *US Navy Gunboats 1885–1945*, Oxford: Osprey Publishing (2021)
Herder, Brian Lane, *US Navy Protected Cruisers 1883–1918*, Oxford: Osprey Publishing (2023)
Karnow, Stanley, *In Our Image: America's Empire in the Philippines*, New York: Random House (1989)
Leeke, Jim, *Manila and Santiago: The New Steel Navy in the Spanish-American War*. Annapolis, MD: Naval Institute Press (2009)
Menton, Linda K. & Tamura, Eileen, *A History of Hawaii, Student Book, Second Edition*, Honolulu: Curriculum Research & Development Group, University of Hawai'i (1999)
Millet, F. D., *The Expedition to the Philippines*, New York: Harper & Brothers (1899)
Montojo, Almirante, *Official Report on the Battle of Manila Bay*, Madrid: El Imparcial (1898)
Nofi, Albert A., *The Spanish-American War, 1898*, Conshohocken, PA: Combined Books (1996)
Sargent, Commander Nathan, USN, *Admiral Dewey and the Manila Campaign*, Washington, DC: Naval Historical Foundation (1947)
Secretary of the Navy, *Annual Report of the Navy Department, 1898*, US Navy (1898)
Secretary of War, *Annual Report of the War Department, 1898*, US Army (1898)
Secretary of War, *Annual Report of the War Department, 1899*, US Army (1899)
Wilcox, Marion, ed., *Harper's History of the War in the Philippines*, New York: Harper and Brothers (1990)
Wilson, Herbert Wrigley, *The Downfall of Spain, Naval History of the Spanish-American War*, London: Sampson Low, Marston and Company (1900)
Wolff, Leon, *Little Brown Brother: How the United States Purchased and Pacified the Philippines*, Garden City, New York: Doubleday (1961)
Rand-McNally Map of Manila Harbor, Chicago: Rand, McNally, Co. Map Publishers (1898)
Websites
https://archives.gov
https://www.history.navy.mil
https://www.loc.gov
https://www.navsource.org/
http://philippineamericanwar.webs.com
https://www.spanamwar.com

INDEX

Figures in **bold** refer to illustrations.

Aguinaldo, General Emilio **12**, **35**
  and army organization 30
  background and character 21
  and Philippine Revolution 11–14, 34, 64
  relationship with US 35, 62–63
  and Spanish–American War 39, 60, 62–63, 73, 75–76, 81, 83, 85–88, 89
  US captures 91
Alapan, battle of (1898) 63, **64**, 65
Anderson, Brigadier-General Thomas M. **73**
  background and character 19
  and insurgents 89
  and Philippine land invasion 65, 66, 72–75, 82, 84
Argos 24, **50–51**, 52
armament and weapons
  Filipino 30
  Spanish 23–24, 25, **26**
  US 27–28, 29, 38, 57
Audaz 24, 69, 70
Augustin y Dávila, Basilio **17**
  background and character 17
  and defense of Manila 58, 60, 61, 75
  plans 32
  and Spanish–American War 39, 57
Australia 66, **66**, 72

Baltimore, USS **27**
  at Manila Bay 40, 41, 44, **50–51**, 52, 56, 57, 59
  overview 28
  and Spanish–American War 37, 38–39, 60, 83
Biak-na-Bato, Pact of (1897) 34, **35**
Blount, James H. 21, 30, 35, 81
Bonifacio y de Castro, General Andrés 11, 12, 13
Boston, USS **28**
  and Hawai'i 8–9
  at Manila Bay 40, 41, 43, **50–51**, 52, 56, 57
  overview 28
  and Spanish–American War 74, 80, 83
Britain 34, 38, 61, 70, 85, 88
Brutus 70, 82
Buenos Aires 24, 69

Caballo 22, 41
Cadarso, Capitan Luis 49, 56
Calkins, Lieutenant 41, 44
Callao 28, 60–61, 83
Cámaro y Libermoore, Contraalmirante Manuel de la 18, 69–70, **69**, 71, 74–75
Cañacao 22, 52
Castilla
  at Manila Bay 43, **50–51**, 52–53, 58, 59
  overview 23
  and Spanish–American War 39
Cavite 43–58, **60**, 63, 72–73
Cervera, Contraalmirante Pascual **69**, 71
Charleston, USS 28, 66–68, **68**, 72, 83, **84**
Chichester, Captain 61, 85
City of Peking 66, **66**, 72
City of Sydney 66, **66**, 72
Concord, USS
  at Manila Bay 40, 41, 43, **50–51**, 53, 57
  overview 28
  and Spanish–American War 37, 84
Corregidor 22, 41, **42**, 59, **64**
Creagh, Chief Yeoman Merrick W. 40
Cuba 14–15, 32, 33, 65, 69, 71

Dewey, Rear Admiral George **20**
  background and character 19
  on Filipinos 21
  and insurgents 35, 62–63, 73, 89
  at Manila Bay 40–58, 40
  and Manila blockade 59–61
  and Montojo 18
  and Spanish–American War 37–40, 70
  and US capture of Philippines 73–74, 75, 76, 80, 81, 82, 83, 84–89
Diederichs, Vizeadmiral Ernst Otto von 61, **63**, 73–74, 82, 85
Dole, Sanford B. 8, 58–59
Don Antonio del Ulloa 23, 43, **50–51**, 52–53, **52**, 58
Don Juan de Austria 23, 43, **50–51**, 52, 57, 58
Dyer, Captain Nehemiah 27, 41

El Cano 24, **50–51**
El Fraile 22, 41, **42**
Ellicott, Lieutenant 40, 45, 88
Emperador Carlos V 69, 70, **70**
empires
  in Southeast Asia **10**
  Spanish 6
  US 6–7, **7**

Faust, Karl Irving 11, 65, 74, 84
Ferguson, Samuel **40**
Filipino forces 30
  commanders 20–21
  overview 29–30
  plans 34–35
  and Spanish–American War 38, 39, 60, 61, 62–63, 73, 75–76, 81, 82–83, 85–88, 89, 91
Fort San Antonio Abad
  armament 26
  and battle of Manila 83, 85, **85**, 86–87, 88
  and "Battle in the Rain" 76, 77, 78–79

Fort Santiago **26**, 89
fortifications 25–26, **26**
France 61

General Lezo 24, 43, **50–51**, 52, 57
Germany
  attitude to Philippines 60
  in Manila Bay 61, 62, 64, 73–74, 82, 85
Greene, Brigadier-General Francis Vinton 20, 74–76, **75**, 82, 85
Gridley, Captain Charles Vernon
  background and character 19
  at Manila Bay 41, 43, 44, 45, 48, 49, 57
  on Spanish Navy 23
Guam 66–68, **67**, **68**, 90

Hawai'i 7–9, 58–59, 66, 72, 90, **91**

Immortalité, HMS 61, 85, 88
Intramuros 25–26, 82, 84, 88, **89**, 93
Irene, SMS 61, **64**, 73–74
Isla de Cuba 23–24, 43, 49, **50–51**, 52, 57, 58
Isla de Luzón 23–24, 49, **50–51**, 52, 57, 58

Japan 61
Jáudenes y Álvarez, Fermín 17, 81, 82, **82**, 88

Kalākaua, King of Hawai'i 8

Lili'uokalani, Queen of Hawai'i 8, 9, **9**
Llanera, General Mariano 12, 35
Long, John D. **34**
  background and character 18
  and Cuba 69, 71
  and Guam 66
  plans 33
  and Spanish–American War 38, 60, 62, 63
Luzon 32, 34

MacArthur, Brigadier-General Arthur, Jr. 20, 81, 82, **82**
McCulloch, USRC
  at Manila Bay 40, 41, 43, **50–51**, 58
  overview 28
  and Spanish–American War 60, 62, 62, 83
McDougall, John A. **40**
McKinley, William **19**
  background and character 18
  and Cuba 15
  and Hawai'i 9, 72
  plans 33
  and Spanish–American War 60, 62
Manila
  defenses and fortifications 22–23, **23**, 25–26, **26**

95

siege and blockade 39, 58, 59–63
US captures 75–89
Manila 24, 50–51, 52, 57
Manila, battle of (1898) **64**, 82–89, **86–87**, **88**
Manila Bay, battle of (1898)
    action 40–58
Marques del Duero 24, 43, **50–51**, 52, **52**, 57, 58
Merritt, Major-General Wesley **21**, 76
    background and character 20
    and Philippine land invasion 65, 74–75, 81, 82, 84–89
    and US plans 33
Mindanao **50–51**, 53
mines 22–23, 41
Monadnock, USS 28, 70, **74**, 75
Monet, General Ricardo 34, 62
Monterey, USS
    overview 28
    and Spanish–American War 62, 70, 72, 74, 75, 82, 83–84
Montojo y Pasarón, Contraalmirante Patricio **18**
    background and character 17–18
    at Manila Bay 43, 45–58
    after Manila Bay 59
    and Manila defenses 22–23
    Subic Bay abandoned by 39–40

Nanshan 28, 38, 43, **50–51**
Noriel, General Mariano 21, 75, 85–88

Olympia, USS **27**, **37**, **38**
    battle ensign 41
    at Manila Bay 40–52, **40**, **44**, **46–47**, **50–51**, **56**, 57, 58
    overview 27
    and Spanish–American War 37, 60, 61, 83, 84–85, 88
Osada 24, 69, 70

Panama Canal 90
Panay 24, 69
Paris, Treaty of (1898) 90
Paterno, Pedro 13, **35**
Patriota 24, 69
Pearl Harbor 8
Pelayo 24, 69, 70, **71**
Petrel, USS
    at Manila Bay 40, 41, 43, 50–51, 52–53, 57, **57**, 58
    overview 28
    and Spanish–American War 37, 83, 85
Philippine–American War (1899–1901) 91
Philippine Revolution (1896–98) 9–14, 60, 61–63, **64**, 73, 75–76, 81–83, 85–88, 89, 91
Philippines
    defenses and fortifications 23–24, **23**, 25–26, **26**

ethnic mix and religion 11
flags **13**, **81**
history and geography 9–14, 20–21
independence 92
insurgents 9–14, 60–63, 73, 75–76, 81, 82–83, 85–88, 89, 91
later history 91–92
Spanish plans for 32
US land invasion **64**, 65–66, 72–89, **86–87**
US plans for 33, 35
Polavieja, General Camilo 12, 13
Proserpina 24, 69, 70
Puerto Rico 33, 69, 90

Rain, Battle in the (1898) **64**, 75–81, **77**, **78–79**
Raleigh, USS
    at Manila Bay 40, 41, 50–51, 52, 53, 57
    overview 28
    and Spanish–American War 60, 61, 73, 83
Rapido 24, 69
Reina Cristina **24**
    at Manila Bay 43, 45–49, **50–51**, 53, **53**, 54–55, 58
    overview 23
Reina Mercedes **24**
Rizal, José 11, **11**, 12
Roosevelt, Theodore 18–19, 34, 37, 70

Sampson, Rear Admiral William T. 69, 71
Sangley Point 22, 43, 45, 52–53
Schley, Commodore Winfield Scott 69, 71
ships
    definition of monitors 72
    overview of Spanish 23–24
    overview of US 27–29
Spain
    and Cuba 14–15
    history and empire 6
    and Philippine Revolution 9–14
    US threats to homeland 70–71
    war's effects on 90
Spanish–American War (1898)
    action 37–89
    origins 5–15
    outbreak 15
    peace treaty 90
    plans 32–35
Spanish Army 24–25, **25**
Spanish forces
    commanders 17–18
    overview 22–26
    plans 32
Spanish Navy 23–24
    Escuadrón del Pacífico 23–24, 39–40, 43–58

Segundo Escuadrón 24, 32, 69–70, 71, 74–75
Subic Bay 39–40, **39**, 73, 92
Suez Canal 69–70, **71**

telegraph cables 60, **61**

United States
    and Cuba 14–15, 33, 65, 69, 71
    and Hawai'i 58–59, 66, 72, 90, **91**
    influence in Pacific 7–9
    overview and imperialism 6–7, **7**
    war's effects on 90–91
US Army Philippines Expedition
    Fifth Corps 69
    2nd Division 82, 84, 85, 88, **88**
    First Brigade 82, 84, 85, 88
    Second Brigade 82, 84, 85, 88, **88**
    1st California Volunteers 72, 74, 78–79
    1st Colorado Volunteers 74, 76, 78–79, 85, 88
    1st Idaho Volunteers 81
    1st Nebraska Volunteers 74, 76
    1st North Dakota Volunteers 81
    1st Wyoming Volunteers 81
    2nd Oregon Volunteers 72, 84, 88
    3rd Artillery 76, 78–79, 81
    6th Artillery 29
    10th Pennsylvania Volunteers 74, 76, 80
    13th Minnesota Volunteers 81
    14th Infantry 65, 72
    18th Infantry 74, 76, 81
    23rd Infantry 74, 81
    Astor Battery 81
US forces
    commanders 18–20
    overview 26–29
    plans 32–34
US Naval War College **33**
US Navy (USN) 26–29
    First Philippine Expedition 65–68, 72–75
    Second Philippine Expedition 74–77, 77–78
    Third Philippine Expedition 75, 81
    Asiatic Squadron 26–28, 32–33, 37–62, 75
    Covering Squadron 71
    Eastern Squadron 70–71

Velasco 23, 43, **50–51**, 52

weapons *see* armament and weapons
Wilcox Rebellion (1895) 9
Williams, Oscar F. 30, 38, 39

Zafiro 28, 38, 43, **50–51**
Zapote Bridge, battle of (1897) 12, **12**

96